Dolphin Borne

by carlos eyles

Watersport Publishing, Inc.
Post Office Box 83727 • San Diego, CA 92138

Printed in the USA

International Standard Book Number (ISBN): 0-922769-25-7

Library of Congress Catalog Card Number: 94-61787
Eyles, Carlos
    Dolphin Borne

Other books by Carlos Eyles
    Diving Free
    Sea Stalking
    the Last of the Blue Water Hunters
    Sea Shadows
    Secret Seas

Cover illustration by Margery Spielman

Acknowledgments

I wish to express my thanks to Ken Loyst for his loyalty and faith in my work, and to Terry Slusher for her design of this book and her steadfast accountability, that it measure up to her high standards. Warm thanks are also due to David Michael Smith, for his inspiration as well as his painstaking edits of the final draft.

For Steve DeWitt, Gary Adkison,
Pat Troy, Michael Menduno, Greg Bravard,
Jordon, and Phil Compton.

The journey is never alone.

With speed He flew to my relief,
As on a radiant dolphin borne;
Awful, yet bright, as lightning shone
The face of my Deliverer God.
— Herman Melville

❖ 1 ❖

THE MUD FLATS BELOW SEEMED ENDLESS. Andy McCorkin's gaze swept across the dry, vacuous tributaries which spread across the flats like flowered nerve endings. Soon patches of white appeared, stark against the dark earth, indicating the beginnings of salt deposits. The plane sped south and the patches thickened to a calcimine blanket that stretched to the far mountains in the west. The Gulf of California's twenty foot tides were never more in evidence than from four miles above sea level. McCorkin pressed his clean-shaven, nearly whiskerless face to the glass and craned a neck that was short and muscular, and seemed to root out of his overly broad shoulders. And though his chest was as deep as a man who toiled daily for his wages, McCorkin's soft hands and scrubbed good looks belied such a notion. He was unworn and scarcely used, and appeared much younger than twenty six years. Below, wind rippled, slate colored water lapped at the cloak of white. This is where it begins, he thought, leaning back into his seat, inhaling a deep breath, more to confirm his presence in the plane than to breathe.

The water was khaki color when he looked again. The Gulf, as it was casually referred to, was changing color at every glance; from olive-brown, to tan, to ocher, to jade, all swirling together at times. Finally, miles from its beginning, a distinct line of gray/blue appeared, separating the tidal waters from the fresh body that ran eight hundred miles down the Gulf where it merged with the Pacific.

McCorkin sat stiffly in his seat. The events of the day had come rapid and unexpected, and he was again piecing them together in an attempt to make some sense of it before he called Cynthia.

"Up ahead," said a balding man in glasses sitting next to him, "is the town of San Felipe." Without replying McCorkin leaned into the window and saw low lying buildings edging the eastern shoreline of the peninsula. "Ever been there?" asked the man.

Still looking out the window, McCorkin shook his head.

"It's quite a town, or used to be," continued the man. "The high tides ran right into the streets. The entire town was built four feet off the ground, with three foot high curbs ringing the main thoroughfares. It was a wild place thirty years ago. These days civilized money has tamed it down with American style hotels and condos. Kind of a shame really."

San Felipe gave way to sand spits, barren beach and indigo water. McCorkin asked, "You spend much time in Baja?"

"I've been coming down here, off and on since the early sixties. My wife and I run a small shop in Marina del Rey called the Latin Quarter. We specialize in clothes, pottery, and wood carvings from Mexico."

McCorkin nodded at the ironies of travel.

"I know your place. I live next door in Manhatten Beach. This is my first flight down the Gulf."

"Well, this must be quite an adventure for you."

"I'm on my way to Bahia de la Ventana to do some diving. I've been down by car twice before. Last fall we drove into Gonzaga, and in the spring in went to San Francisquito.

"That can be a nasty road into Gonzaga from the north."

"I heard it was. We came in from the south. That was no picnic. Mostly riverbed and burro trail. It was the worst road I've ever been on."

"In the sixties and before, you'd hardly call them roads. But whenever we got bogged down I'd think, thank God for these terrible roads. It's the only thing that keeps the Americans out of Baja. A small price for unspoiled beauty. Up until the time the main road was completed back in '73, the peninsula and its waters were as wild has any stretch of land or sea in the world. You're seeing the last of a country as God made it."

McCorkin turned to the window for a look at God's handiwork. Save for a dirt thread of a road that appeared out of a canyon and seemed to go nowhere, the red volcanic mountains to the west and the deep emerald waters bordered thinly in white sand gave no indication that man had laid a hand upon His creation. The scrub bush countryside was not unlike the California desert and he thought of Cynthia. They were to have hiked into the high desert for the weekend and do some camping. He'd completely forgotten about it. They had gone last year in the spring when the desert flowers were in full bloom.

"That'd be Puertecitos," said the man pointing past McCorkin to the window, "you should be able to see the islands of the Midriff."

McCorkin leaned into the window and the island called Salvatierra laid off to the east like a piece of rough hewn brick set in turquoise. For a spearfisherman, even those with McCorkin's limited experience, the sighting of an island quickened the pulse; an atavistic response to a wilderness that lay hidden, and in waiting, beneath the surface. The island beckoned from twenty thousand feet.

Further south and east rose an island so large it reduced the Mid-riff chain to scattered stones. "Is that Guardian Angel?" asked McCorkin, pointing to its northern tip.

"That it is," said the man without looking. "It's the longest island in the Gulf, forty-two miles. They say its infested with rattlesnakes. There's the myth that the Indians carried them over to protect caches of gold they hid from the Spaniards. No gold has ever been found, but there's still a hell of a lot of rattlesnakes. I understand that just ten years ago the fish population was extraordinary; like flies on a fresh cow turd. Now its completely fished out, nothing. It was the road that did it."

McCorkin inspected the island's shoreline as it sailed by, noting the points that ranged out to sea, holding promises it could no longer keep. He had heard the big fish stories of Guardian Angel. It was the place to go fifteen years ago. Now one had to travel to the peninsula's end, Bahia de la Ventana, and Cerralvo island to find the big fish.

The bald headed man pointed off across the peninsula into the western horizon.

"You can just make out the hook of the bay that hides Scammon's lagoon. It looks like a sliver of blue separating the land."

"Isn't that where the gray whales go every year?"

"Yep, one year they mate, and the next they calve, then mate again the following year."

"Why's it called Scammon's lagoon? I heard it was named after the guy who started protecting the whales?"

"Hardly. Scammon was a whaler, and a rather greedy one at that. No one really knows how he found the gray whale's breeding grounds, hidden as it was from the sea. But he found it, and once inside, the whales were easy prey in those close quarters. After the first harpoonings the whales turned on the boats to defend themselves, something they rarely do. They broke up dories and nearly killed a couple of men. It took Scammon a week to repair the dories and come up with a better plan. He decided to anchor in shallow on a sand spit next to a deep channel and gun the whales down with a bomb lance as they drifted by. Killed alot of whales he couldn't retrieve, but the plan worked, and he filled the mother ship in record time. Wanting the lagoon for himself he agreed to keep the same crew working on shares, and swore them all to secrecy. Back in San Francisco, the other whalers thought he had just got lucky, because it usually took years to fill a boat and he'd done it in less than a month. When he returned from a second trip loaded to the gunwales with whale oil and bone they knew it was no fluke, and half the fleet was waiting to follow him down a third time. He tried to lose them. And for a time he did and slipped into the lagoon without being seen. But the fleet smelled him out, literally. The stench of drying blubber gave him away. The whalers followed the wind right to the lagoon. Once inside they took up the massacre. The gray whales put a lot of dories down before it was over, but they were overwhelmed by the bomb lances. The slaughter went on for several years, then the whales vanished. It was believed that the whalers had wiped them out, and that the grays had become extinct. Actually the whales had changed their migration routes from Baja to Korea. At least that's the theory, and there's some evidence to support it. The grays found in Korean waters during that time were very belligerent and ready to attack any and all whaling vessels that came their way. They knew the difference between a whaler and a fishing boat, and built quite a reputation for themselves. They were particularly dangerous during breeding and calving. Years later the development of petroleums and lubricants all but wiped out the whaling industry in America, and Scammons lagoon was forgotten. Then at some point the whales began to return. Fortunately, they were rediscovered by naturalists whose interest was in their preservation and were ultimately given sanctuary."

McCorkin listened to the story while eyeing the strip of blue he thought to be Scammon's lagoon. When the man had finished he turned and asked, "do you think whales are as intelligent as humans?"

"I don't know. Dr. John Lilly, who worked with dolphins for as long as anyone, believed that their intelligence was beyond our comprehension. Dolphins and whales have been around a hell of a lot longer than humans. Who knows?"

McCorkin looked back to the window for the slice of blue, but it had vanished.

Yeah, who knows anything, he thought.

The eastern edge of the peninsula slid by, occasionally marked by bits of cleared land and huts indicating man's meager hold on the terrain. "I don't see how anyone can survive down there," said McCorkin. "They gotta be awfully tough people."

"Indian tough. The Jesuits tried to establish themselves here in 1697, and had a hell of a time. Although they built twenty-one missions over a hundred and fifty year period, it was rough going. They finally gave up. The country was too hard, even for the Catholics. They say the Baja Indian was as tough an Indian who ever lived. There's a legend of a tribe, actually seven tribes, that existed here in the 12th century. They've found cave paintings and mummified body parts that indicate these Indians were over seven feet tall. Apparently they were hunters and followed the game down the peninsula to its tip. From there they crossed over by canoe and raft to the shores of Mexico. They conquered every tribe that came their way. There's the belief that Baja could well have been the cradle of a remarkably tough and perhaps important civilization."

"So what happened to those tribes?"

"Who knows. Just disappeared."

Santa Rosalia and its iron works whisked by, then came Mulege and its oasis of greenery fed by a spring spawned river. McCorkin gave the picturesque town a passing glance as Conception Bay, with its serpentined inlets and coves and jigsawed inner islands fell into view. Spectacular from the air, Conception Bay looked to be a spearfisherman's paradise, but it too had gone the way of Guardian Angel and the islands of the north. There were a few spots left, but it was unlikely McCorkin would ever find them. Those who knew them kept their secrets well. How can a place like this be so filled with life for millions of years, thought McCorkin, then change so drastically in fifteen years? It's like I'm chasing time in this plane. Every minute equals a hundred years. Will I get to Bahia de la Ventana in time? Will I be a minute too late?

The plane sped south, shadowing time. McCorkin reclined into his seat and closed his eyes.

He dreamed he was floating in purple/blue water that was very deep. After a time he noticed that the water had become a brownish red, and it caused him to stop floating and tread water. Something was wrong. The water turned a dark red and seemed thicker. It pooled about him and he tried to swim away, but he always remained in its center. He lifted his hand and the water ran from his fingers as blood. He swam in thrashing strokes attempting to separate himself from the blood/water. A dolphin appeared and began to circle the red stained water. He reached for its fin but couldn't get a grip, the slick blood preventing a clean grasp. Again and again he tried to catch hold of the dorsal fin, and each time it slipped away. He knew the dolphin was trying to help him, but for some reason it couldn't penetrate the blood/water. He became fatigued, and struggling to stay afloat, floundered weakly in the blood. He was startled awake by the words, "La Paz," and sat bolt upright.

"I thought you'd want to see it from the air," said the man apologetically.

The dolphin swam in McCorkin's eyes as he followed a pointing finger to the window. A crowded, smoking city had replaced the desolate countryside, and the brilliant blue waters of the Gulf had turned pea green and was cramped with boats at anchor. The plane banked steeply and took with it the last images of the dream. McCorkin's stomach lifted, but it came not from the motion of the plane but from the nearness of his destination. The plane settled into its landing pattern over dilapidated shacks, dusty laundry, and abandoned cars, briefly filling him with Mexico's third world poverty.

Inside the terminal, arrangements were made to fly to Bahia de la Ventana, and then, having a half hour to wait, McCorkin made a call to Cynthia in Los Angeles; she'd be home by now.

"Yes, I'll accept operator," came her soft, sure, voice, which abruptly changed to mock anger," "Andy! Where're you calling from?"

"La Paz, babe. La Paz, Baja California. I tried calling you at the office before I left, but they said you were out on a presentation."

"I was with Mitchell down on Wilshire. What are you doing in La Paz?"

"You won't believe it. I got a call at seven this morning from a guy in the Blue Fins spearfishing club. There was an opening for a trip that was leaving today. This guy got sick and bailed, and I picked up his ticket."

"And how did you manage the time off?"

"My territory is tight right now. Bernie gave me three days vacation time. Including the weekend I'll get five days, which I'll stretch to six if the diving is good."

"Andy," said Cynthia, her voice rising in plea, "the way you keep chipping the days away there won't be anything left for us by the time summer rolls around."

"Don't worry, babe, I can always squeeze Bernie for a few more days. We'll have plenty of time.

"Are you diving there in La Paz?"

"No, a place called Bahia de la Ventana. It's down near the tip of the peninsula. I'll be picking up a shuttle in a few minutes. You remember me mentioning Ray Messias, one of the all time great spearfisherman? He lives down here. I'll be diving with him and two other big timers, Jeremy Hall and Frank Scolari. It's a once in a lifetime thing. I couldn't pass it up. A boat is all lined up. It'll be great."

"Andy, please be careful, don't try and be a hero or anything."

"Don't worry, Babe, it's going to be fantastic. I'll bring you back a present."

"Just bring back yourself." Cynthia said between sighs. "I love you."

"I love you too, babe. See you Monday or Tuesday. I'll call you when I get in."

Fifteen minutes later McCorkin boarded the shuttle for the twenty minute flight. Enroute the dolphin dream flashed back in undertones of disturbing images, but when the plane rose over a hump of a low mountain range, and the blue waters of the Gulf reappeared with Cerralvo Island seeming to be but a stones throw from the shoreline, all thoughts of the dream vanished.

❖ 2 ❖

McCORKIN LEANED AGAINST THE STARBOARD gunwales of the twenty-four foot power boat, Pescadora, and aimed an uncocked speargun down the center of the gangway to which the boat was end-tied. An imaginary grouper of immense proportions drifted beyond the range of the speargun. Unconsciously he held his breath and focused on a spot just behind the grouper's gill plate. A light punch to his shoulder startled him into an exhale, and he lowered the speargun.

"Jesus, he should have been here by now." Jeremy Hall had come from below deck and was looking down the same gangway that a moment before held the waters of McCorkin's mind. Bearded and deeply tanned, Hall's face was pinched into a scowl, he moved with impatience. "Let me know the second he shows up."

The gray, close cropped head of Frank Scolari leaned out of the companionway. He smiled through dark tinted sun glasses, "Relax Jerry. When has Ray ever been on time? He'll be along."

Hall frowned, "It's already one o'clock. We've lost half the fucking day."

McCorkin laid the speargun next to the other long guns that leaned against the transom, and looked out onto the sparkling, wind-rippled bay. Although early in May, the Mexican sun blazed with midsummer intensity, and he wore a bright blue tee shirt to protect a day old sunburn, acquired in the vain attempt to blend in with the weathered browns of his companions. Despite the calm waters of the bay, he walked to the port gunwales with a hint of unsteadiness and leaned his thighs against them for support. His gaze ran to the mouth of the bay then out to Cerralvo island which, in the crystalline air, appeared nearer than it actually was, rising out of an expanse of blue like a chunk of weathered bloodstone.

Cerralvo lay eighteen miles due south from the small natural harbor of Bahia de la Ventana. In recent years the bay shore of this century old fishing village had been made over into a marina, complete with a boat launching ramp and a fuel dock. Which, along with an air strip, and El Presidente Inn, accommodated the Americans that flew down in the fall, winter and spring to fish these southern most waters. The sterile cleanliness of the marina lay in sharp contrast to the tattered hovels of the dust blown fishing village, like an artificial limb attached to the hip of a worn-out derelict.

These waters sparkled in a light different from that of the northern waters and dazzled McCorkin with its pristine radiance. Pelicans, gulls, and terns fell from the sky like candy from a broken pinata on water that continually flowered in glittery eruptions of bait fish, brought to the surface by pursuing jacks and mackerel. The sky swirled with life, and the sea jumped with promises of things to come. McCorkin awaited at its threshold, living his outrageous dream, moving cautiously, afraid of awakening.

Raymond Messias stepped onto the gangway and looked down its one hundred and fifty foot length. The Pescadora was tied at its end, and McCorkin's blue shirted back vibrated in waiting. The boat slips on either side of the gangway held all manner of vessels; cabin cruisers, trawlers, pangas, fly-bridged marlin boats, and sailboats. Carrying a duffel bag, cumbersome dive gear bag, and two long wooden spearguns, Messias surefootedly made his way down the floating finger of unpainted wood. Near the halfway point a reflected glint of light caught his left peripheries. Three men stood on the foredeck of a fishing trawler tied in its slip on the next gangway. One of the men was aiming a rifle at Messias' head. Instinctively Messias dropped to the deck, seeking cover behind the bow of a marlin boat, his gear clattering on the rough wooden planking. Uproarious laughter brought him partially off the deck.

"No es problema señor. No le vamos a mater usted. No es Tiburon," shouted one of the men, their laughter soaring to new heights. Messias rose from the gangway, nodding his head in a slow menacing way. The shark fisherman swayed drunkenly on the whitewashed trawler, its green gunwales chipped and gauged and cleaved of wood where the sharks had been hauled aboard.

Shark fishermen were the same the world over, thought Messias, picking up the scattered gear; men who eventually became what they hunt.

McCorkin had turned at the noise of the crashing gear, and saw a man rise and turn to stare across the next gangway. McCorkin knew that something untoward had caused him to hit the deck. Then he saw the long guns, and knew that the man was Raymond Messias.

McCorkin leaned down into the companion way.

"He's here!"

Jeremy Hall came out on the aft deck muttering complaints about the afternoon wind. Frank Scolari, still below, switched on the batteries, came topside, turned a key, and brought the engine to life.

Messias moved agilely with his cumbersome load down the gangway. Short of six feet, with the beginnings of a paunch, his waistline and thinning brown hair put his age to be around forty. The hair was slicked back on a head that looked small, sitting as it was on overly broad shoulders. The face, dark and Greek, was oval with a wide expressive mouth. Dark brown eyes set deep and close together gave him an intense, almost cross-eyed look.

McCorkin eagerly extended his hand, "Hi, I'm Andy McCorkin."

Messias measured the muscular young man with golden curls and earnest blue eyes, then handed him the largest of the two bags he was carrying, "Ray Messias."

"What happened down on the gangway?" asked McCorkin.

"A couple of shark fisherman were waving a rifle around."

"Were they serious?"

"No, just drunk."

Jeremy Hall stepped around McCorkin and reached for Messias' duffel bag, "Where the hell have you been? We've been here since six thirty."

"Been here since '81." Said Messias, flatly ignoring Hall's attempt at a reprimand.

"We gotta get moving. We're only going to get a couple of hours of water time." Hall set the duffel bag down and reached for the long guns that Messias had cradled under an arm.

Messias followed the guns on board, taking Scolari's hand in the generous grip of an old friend "How ya doin' Frank?"

Scolari smiled "fish sticking time, Ray," and then went forward to tend the bow line. McCorkin untied the stern line, and when all dock lines were free, Hall expertly maneuvered the cruiser out of its close quarters, and idled to the mouth of the breakwater. Messias, taking this last opportunity of smooth water, went below to change into shorts and a tee shirt.

After clearing the short jetty that fingered the west end of the bay, Hall kicked the engine up to 2600 rpms and the Pescadora leaped into a two-foot chop that came out of the northwest. Scolari sat beside Hall in the only other seat available. Messias with folded arms, stood between the two seats, and McCorkin clung to the back of Scolari's seat.

"The last two days the winds have been blowing thirty-five knots," said Messias. "Today is the first time it's settled down enough to make a run. There's still a fair swell running on the outside. The Mexicans say this could be the only break we'll have. Another storm is due in a day or two."

"Did you get any reports on visibility or currents?" questioned Scolari.

"No one has left the marina," continued Messias, "including the Mexicans. The currents are probably as bad as always. I hope the visibility has held up."

"Are the currents strong off this island?" asked McCorkin.

"They can get up to six and seven knots on the outside," explained Scolari. "You've got to be continually aware of where you are."

Messias left his position between the seats and walked to the plunging bow of the boat. McCorkin marveled at the ease with which he moved, and wondered how many times he had made a trip such as this, probably hundreds. McCorkin moved to Messias' vacated spot between the seats and asked Scolari, "What section of the island are we going to dive?"

"Good question. I don't know. What do you think, Ray?" shouted Scolari to Messias standing in the bow. "Do we have enough time to work the back side?"

"Let's go around the corner and see what it looks like," answered Messias. "We can work the southeast tip if the visibility has held. There's a couple of good pargo spots on the inside. I could work that deep reef southwest of the tip, and you take that hundred yard reef further west. Saw some nice fish there on the east end last fall. If the current has pushed the fish down, we'll jump back into the boat and drift for amberjack along the drop offs."

"Sounds like the plan." Said Scolari, nodding in agreement.

Pinched out of the conversation, McCorkin alternately stared at the island and at the back of Raymond Messias. Until this moment he hadn't fully comprehended the arena he was about to enter. It was as though he had awakened from an all night drunk, and had to recall exactly what route had been traveled that placed him in these circumstances.

The trip to Gonzaga nearly a year ago was the turning point. Up until then he had been content to spear small fish along the California coastline during the summer months. In those few years he had developed a general sense of the ocean, and a degree of confidence in his abilities to operate in those shallow waters. When an invitation was extended to dive Gonzaga in the Gulf, there was no reason to believe he wasn't up to it. However, the waters of the Gulf were not the genial waters of the California coast line. He was unprepared for its powerful fish, wild currents, and deep dives required to find fish. Though he saw no sharks, tales of their sightings were gleefully reported by the experienced hunters and had him on edge throughout his stay. In two days of diving he managed to spear several cabrillo, and a small yellow-tail, and considered himself fortunate to have accomplished that feat. Despite the faltering beginning, the Gulf intrigued him. He returned to the States, acquired a big game speargun, and rigged it to specifically handle the powerful, deep water fish. Six months later he was diving San Francisquito where the water was clear, and the fish plentiful. The first day he lost the new speargun after spearing a large grouper that had charged off and run the line across rocks, eventually severing it and taking the gun to the depths. Using a lighter rig, he was forced to hunt for smaller fish and was not obliged to stay up with the other, more experienced divers. In truth, the fish he speared, though small by Gulf standards, extended the limits of his fledgling skills, and the depth more than once tested his courage. McCorkin had long been seeking an arena that would call for, physical strength, and demand a certain kind of mental toughness. Big game spearfishing had become the arena, yet beyond all the challenges that were presented, it was the spector of sharks that compelled him. For his fear of them was unlike any fear he had ever known as a boy or man. And their images forever played behind his eyes. Invariably, he would see them materializing out of the deep water where an instant before there was nothing. They would sweep behind him in flashing blurs, unseen, but always felt. He would turn in a rush to face them and the water would always be empty. A blue nothingness, full of ghosts. He interpreted his fears as a terrible flaw, a weakness of character that he was determined to exorcise.

Submitting his name to the few and scattered spearfishing clubs in California, he made himself available for any expeditions into the Gulf. But never, in his most elaborate fantasies did he include himself in the company of Jeremy Hall, Frank Scolari, and the legendary Raymond Messias. Up until yesterday he had only heard their names in whispered reverence. Now he was enroute with them to some faraway island whose bursting waters produced the grandest fish in all the Gulf.

McCorkin's eyes were riveted on the island that rose out of the sea like a great purple monolith. While Messias moved freely about the boat, McCorkin held fast to the seats, his imagination flying unchecked into head to head confrontations with the sharks of Cerralvo Island.

Messias came aft, and with brown, square hands, opened up his gear bag. A white rubber boat fender, two feet long and six inches in diameter, was lifted out and laid on the deck. Attached to the fender was a hundred and fifty feet of yellow, polyurethane line. The other end of the line was connected to ten feet of twelve strand stainless steel cable. He unscrewed the two barbed detachable spear point from the spear shaft, which laid in the groove of the five-and-a-half-foot long laminated teak and mahogany speargun, and dropped a slide ring, to which the cable was looped and crimped, around the naked end of the spear shaft. Then replaced the spear point, spinning it down an inch of threads. The cable ran from the spear shaft, just above the muzzle, down to the pistol grip, where it looped around a half-inch long finger that connected to the trigger, and released the line simultaneously with the pull of the trigger. The line ran the length of the stock to a small bronze cleat set behind the muzzle, and back down again to the pistol grip, where it was attached to the poly line. The yellow poly line was doubled up and wedged under two thick rubber bands placed around the foot long extension of the stock behind the pistol grip. When the trigger was pulled, the shaft, under three hundred pounds of thrust from the three 9/16" bands of near solid rubber tubing, left the stock much as an arrow leaves a crossbow, and was connected via the poly line to the floating boat fender on the surface.

Messias set the prepared speargun next to the others that were similarly rigged which rested against the transom of the Pescadora. Stepping over to the port railing, he half sat watching McCorkin stiffly fighting off the movement of the boat. After a time he asked, "Have you hunted these waters before, Andy?"

"No, not this far south," replied McCorkin, glad for some conversation. "I dove San Francisquito last fall, and Gonzaga before that. I didn't know what you guys were up to until about a year ago... "

"We don't like to advertise," interrupted Hall, "the hunting grounds are drying up fast enough.

"Is that why you guys keep such a low profile?", asked McCorkin. "Nobody knows you exist."

"It's a secret club," snickered Hall. "Only idiots with ten pound balls are members."

Scolari laughed, "Yeah, in cold water those balls shrivel right up, and if sharks show they fucking disappear."

"You got that right," shouted Hall. "Nobody wants to be down eighty feet holding their breath and looking up at the belly of a hammerhead. Not a whole lot of folks ready to deal with that kind of scene."

"The fact is," interrupted Messias, "nobody really wants to know anything about us. We're throwbacks to another time. Like the American Indian, or the Eskimo. They had a special knowledge of the land, and we have a special knowledge of the water."

"Yeah, look what happened to the fucking Indians," shouted Hall over his shoulder. "Their profile was too high, and boom, elimination."

Messias continued, "We're like a small tribe that's scattered all over the place; down in Florida, California, Australia, Europe. All these tribes of ocean hunters who know their water better than any man or machine has ever known it."

"What about scientists," asked McCorkin. "You know, marine biologists?"

"Scientists take their equipment down to measure the ocean and record it, but they can't see anything beyond their instruments. The technology has dulled their senses. They're looking at needles and gauges, and writing it all down. They can't see the big picture. Look what's happening to the planet. They can't even see the damage unless it shows up on a machine. It doesn't exist unless they can turn it into a "fact".

Messias paused as if to stop but then seemed compelled to continue.

"The most sensitive instrument ever created was man. If he spends his time in a wilderness, whether its the sea or the land, he's going to understand the big picture. How things connect up together."

"Ray's big on connections," interrupted Hall.

"When you're stalking fish, you got to understand the connections," said Messias to no one in particular. "You got to know temperature changes in the water, where the thermocline is, shifts in visibility, sun position, where the bait is, if its been fed on, when it was fed on, what kind of fish was feeding. And everything is changing all the time. Plus you got to know how it effects the type of fish you're hunting. Each set of conditions affects different fish in different ways. When you are holding all this knowledge inside you see the ocean like it was this living thing."

"Who would know all this shit except somebody who was seeing it all the time, year after year," added Scolari. "It's been passed down word of mouth from generation to generation of blue water hunters for the last fifty years. Nothing written, it's all inside of us.'

"That's a lot of knowledge," said McCorkin. "You'd think people would be interested."

"It's not the way it works," offered Scolari, "because in the end they only see us as killers. People don't want to know about the killing."

"Everyone," shouted Hall from the wheel, "wants to believe that fish are swimming around in styrofoam plates covered with cellophane."

"Everyone," said Messias solemnly, "ought to kill their own food for a year."

"Why is that?" Asked McCorkin.

"They'd have a lot more respect for the creatures they ate, and a better understanding of how they're connected to the natural world. Maybe they'd start to see a piece of the big picture."

Messias suddenly became quiet, as if he had revealed more than he wanted to. In the awkward silence Scolari asked McCorkin, "So, did you score any fish in Francisquito?"

"I lost a big grouper and wound up getting some yellowtail and a couple of cabrillo. The fish were everywhere." McCorkin beamed at the memory.

"Don't pull off on that small shit here," chided Hall.

McCorkin's grin dissolved, "Okay, sure."

"There's big fish off this island and they've seen us before," continued Hall. "Don't spook anything before we can scout it out. If you see something with some size, go for it, otherwise back off." Messias, who had continued to scrutinize McCorkin, said, "Andy, you come with me. We'll work away from Jerry and Frank." Without waiting for a reply, Messias turned his back to the three men and faced the ocean. The others fell silent as the southeast end of Cerralvo sharpened into view.

The island rose in vertical, jagged edged escarpments, maroon and primordial out of the white capped sea. Green splashed below ivory dunged cornices and across the barren landscape. Closer inspection revealed the green to be short stands of cactus, dwarfed by the torrid, unyielding environment. Only the birds, who took their sustenance from the sea, found comfort here, resting in volcanic pock marks that honeycombed the island to its tip. Cerralvo provided little in the way of nourishment above the water, but was host to a thriving wilderness below.

Hall swung the boat wide, around the reef studded southeast tip, then ran parallel along the windward shore for five minutes. He slowed to a glide at the entrance of a small cove which was protected from the west winds by a glacier-sized panel of volcanic rock that had broken away from the island and laid a hundred feet out into the water. Scolari went forward to the anchor locker, opened the hatch and pulled out anchor, chain and rode, then waited for the boat to finish its glide, before noiselessly lowering the anchor as Hall backed the boat downwind.

McCorkin looked over the side and could easily make out detail on the twenty foot bottom. Tropical reef fish in brilliant blues and oranges scurried among the rocks, and a school of silver, scalloped-shaped tangs with yellow tails drifted under the boat, nearly obscuring the sea floor. "This water is super clear. Is it always this way?"

"Usually," replied Scolari, pulling a wet suit out of his gear bag, "unless it rains, then the runoff might cloud it up for a day or two."

Costumed in neon, the parading fish held McCorkin's attention, and when finally he broke away from the railing, the others were well on their way to suiting up. Hurriedly, he dug into his gear bag, and pulled out a two piece wet suit of farmer john type bottoms which covered his legs and torso, and a long sleeve, hooded top, followed by a pair of long bladed fins, a mask, snorkel, and gloves. Each item seemed to fuel his tension. In his nervousness he jammed a zipper struggling into the wet suit, then misplaced a bootie, and couldn't locate his weight belt. The closer he came to readiness, the more he fumbled. Hall, Scolari, and Messias were suited and ready for the water in twenty minutes. McCorkin had found the bootie buried in the foot of a swim fin, and was now searching for the lost weight belt. Hall and Scolari swung over the transom, and stood on the swim step.

"Work west, up the island to that long breaking reef," said Messias. "That leaves the deep reef and everything east for me and McCorkin. We've only got a couple of hours. We should be back in the marina before sundown." McCorkin found his weight belt as Hall and Scolari slid into the water. They separated momentarily to cock their spearguns, then kicked west, up the island.

"You ready?" asked Messias who had climbed over the transom and was standing on the swim step. McCorkin, with the snorkel in his mouth, nodded that he was. Messias slipped into the water as McCorkin lifted a leg over the transom. Once on the swim step he crouched low, as the others had done, and eased into the water. The transparent water seemed to bring the schooling fish to within reaching distance, and McCorkin extended his hand to touch them twenty feet away. The aquarium-like water swept away the outside word and all thoughts of it dissolved in visual overload. The snap-crackle sounds of the shallows resounded in castanet accompaniment to the rhythmical weavings of the tropical fish. The shift of environments was as instantaneous as it was complete.

Messias had cocked his speargun and was moving out into deep water. McCorkin, realizing he was alone, extracted himself from the promenading fish and lifted his head to find Messias' churning fins seventy-five feet away moving to the outside. Hastily cocking his speargun, he swam off in pursuit.

A hundred feet from the anchored boat the bottom dropped away and the bustling activities of the shallows were absorbed by eerie blue depths. In the sea chop McCorkin lost sight of Messias and stopped to tread water. A swim fin arched briefly out of the water, then vanished fifty yards away. Swimming toward the disappearing fin, he reached what he guessed to be the general area, and began to search the bottom. He found Messias sixty feet down, crouched low among a cluster of boulders as motionless as the rock on which his speargun rested. Already he had been down for some time so when he lifted from his position, McCorkin assumed that it was to ascend for a breath. Instead, he moved thirty feet east to another boulder and settled behind it.

Under a breath-hold, at a depth of sixty feet, the constructs of time liquify and change with perspective; for McCorkin, time appeared to protract, the seconds becoming minutes and the minutes stretching to an eternity; for Messias, time advanced with such ponderance it could not be discerned at all.

McCorkin sensed this oblique passage of time as he watched Messias from opposite ends of their hourglass.

Finally, Messias made his ascent, causing McCorkin to shake his head in open wonder at such a breath-hold. Arriving on the surface, Messias rounded off the dive, cleared the snorkel of its water, and apart from a few deep inhales, and exhales, showed no physical evidence of the dive. He then tapped McCorkin on the shoulder and pointed down.

McCorkin was not, in any way, prepared to make such a dive. Good sense would have had him decline the offer. Instead he began to hyperventilate. After a minute of deep breathing, he sucked one last breath to capacity, and with a tinge of light-headedness, kicked down to twenty feet and neutral buoyancy. From there, the weight of the water provided the impetus, and he descended in a steep glide towards the bottom. At forty feet the speed of the glide doubled as momentum gathered. With his left hand fixed to the nose of his face mask, he pinched it, forcing air up through the eustachian tubes and into the middle ear, where it equalized the inner pressure with the outside water pressure. At fifty feet the water was several degrees colder, the light dimmer, the water pressure a tangible force, and he was plummeting to the bottom like a cannon ball. Attempting to pull out of the dive, he misjudged its speed, and clumsily crashed to his knees on the sea floor. Breathless after righting himself, it was all he could do to suppress the urge to immediately resurface. He had been down to this depth once before in San Francisquito, but it was at his own convenience where, after a number of previous dives, he was able to comfortably test his limits.

In this cold, dim world, the pressure of the water, and its accompanied psychic pressure brought more than he could bear, and he pushed off the bottom in hurried ascent. The water tonnage aloft held him to the bottom, and in near panic he bent low at the knees and pushed again. This time gaining enough clearance to sweep his legs he lifted onerously off the sea floor. Straining against the compressed atmosphere, his muscled thighs drained oxygen from an already depleted blood stream. Half way to the surface carbon dioxide had built a brick wall in his lungs and thrust him to the edge of incapacitation. The adrenal gland, functioning as it should, drove home a direct shot, gaining him the strength to kick the final twenty feet. He erupted through the surface with a lung wrenching exhale, followed by a dizzying series of gasping breaths.

Messias observed McCorkin's novice display without comment and swam a hundred feet southeast, paralleling the island, and dropped down again. McCorkin followed from the surface, his breaths coming in wheezing gulps. Messias glided fluidly to the bottom and settled, half-hidden behind a boulder. After an interminable wait he lifted from the spot and drifted ahead to another boulder. So smoothly did he move about the depths that McCorkin was reminded of the ease with which top athletes went about their sport, giving the impression that their feats were within the grasp of anyone who dared to make the attempt. Messias moves as though the water doesn't exist, thought McCorkin. It's no more a barrier for him that it is for a seal.

Messias eventually lifted from the boulder and made his way to the surface. Again he tapped McCorkin, and pointed down. McCorkin, whose wind had not yet returned, shook off the invitation with a half smile, unsure if it was not some sort of dark joke.

Messias worked his way east, leaving McCorkin to observe from above. He had made a half dozen dives, and was down again. The movement of his speargun off a boulder alerted McCorkin that something was about. Following the point of the spear twenty feet beyond the boulder, the black shadow of a grouper hovered at the edge of the sand. The fish, every bit as large as Messias, drifted toward him with cautious curiosity. When it was ten feet off the point of the speargun, Messias pulled the trigger. The shaft released and a loud "schunk" resounded through the water. It struck the grouper just above the gill plate and it exploded across the rocky bottom with Messias in tow and was out of sight in seconds. Swimming as fast as he could on the surface, McCorkin tracked the yellow line. Seventy feet away Messias casually made his ascent, the poly line slipping through the fingers of his left hand. He had reached the surface, and was pulling up the slack line when McCorkin arrived. McCorkin had never before witnessed the stalking and spearing of a large fish in such deep water, and when Messias had finished cinching the line to the float, his excitement spilled out.

"That fish is enormous, Ray. How much do you think it weighs?"

"Hard to say, somewhere around ninety pounds. You want to drop down to see how badly it's hung up in the cave while I get my breath back?"

McCorkin, fully rested, and suitably pumped up nodded that he would. Hyperventilating to a dangerous point of dizziness, he sucked in one last breath and dove down the yellow line. Controlling the rate of descent by way of his grip on the line, he reached the sixty foot bottom without incident. Arriving at the cave's entrance, he peered in, paused until his eyes adjusted to the darkness then saw the fish wedged deep into the base of the cave fifteen feet inside the entrance. The size of it nearly filled the cave and seized what little breath McCorkin had left. Withdrawing his head, he pushed hard for the surface and, though less tense on this dive, struggled to extract himself from the pressure that restrained him. Free of the sea floor he slogged steadily to the top.

On the surface, and between gasps, he explained to Messias the position of the fish all the while wondering how he was going to dive to that depth, and physically wrestle a fish that size from the cave on a single breath-hold.

Messias descended down the yellow line, and upon reaching the entrance of the cave disappeared inside. On the surface McCorkin measured time from his end of the hourglass. After an interminable wait the fins of Messias reappeared at the entrance. Then came his legs, and finally his back, bent with effort from pulling out the resisting fish.

When the grouper broke free of the cave Messias turned for the surface, gripping the fish beneath its flared gills. The size of the fish all but obscured him from McCorkin's view. It's breadth was greater than the man, and its length nearly as long. Messias reached the top, and for the first time was laboring in his breaths. Up close the grouper was massive, and McCorkin reached out to touch it as though to confirm what he saw.

"I'm taking this fish back to the boat," said Messias, "then scout a deep reef south of here. Why don't you move inside and look for cabrillo and pargo." McCorkin resisted the advice, for he had not intended to spear small fish. However, this water was decidedly over his head so he nodded affirmatively and swam toward the island. The underwater terrain gradually rose as he neared the shore. In many ways the sea floor mirrored the land; rounded boulders with stumpy, dull, seaweed clinging to their crowns; strings of faded, brown sargasso, growing in sparse clumps like dry weeds in abandoned gardens. The vegetation was not nearly as striking, nor as abundant as the kelp forests of the colder Pacific, but what was lost in lush vegetation was copiously balanced in a rich variety of sea life. Schools of black angel fish, and brilliant yellow butterfly fish parted to comfortable distances when McCorkin made his first dive. No longer obliged to push himself to reckless depths, he settled easily behind an outcropping of rocks in thirty five feet of water. This depth was light, almost airy, compared to the water just thirty feet deeper, which had a weighted darkness to it. Tropical fish which had gracefully avoided his descent now closed to his unattended backside, fluttering an arms length away. McCorkin waited patiently behind a boulder as Messias had done, keeping his attention to the extreme boundaries of the seventy-foot visibility. Clouds of minute, semitransparent fish hovered close to the bottom, breaking up his line of sight and, in places, shutting down the visibility to less than twenty-five feet. Out of breath, and seeing nothing in the way of a decent sized fish, he lifted from behind the boulder and kicked easily to the surface.

At ease with the depth, McCorkin was able to concentrate on the stalking of a fish. In thirty minutes he made a dozen dives, and had glimpses of pargo and cabrillo ranging in size from fifteen to twenty pounds, but could not get close enough for a shot. Fish seen from the surface would swim away as soon as he made his drop, and those on the bottom were never curious enough to investigate his presence. Smaller, five to ten pound cabrillo and snapper were always on the move, coming and going in every direction. Their movements and those of the bait and reef fish were a constant distraction and continually broke up the ocean scene that played before McCorkin. The experienced eye of the Gulf hunter, which could separate movement, and make distinctions in camouflage and detail, were not his. In addition, and of equal importance, his unfamiliarity with the habits and characteristics of these fish gave him no basis for a workable stalking plan. What he did see in spearable fish were their fleeting tails, and he had no idea from where they came, nor to where they disappeared.

A large pargo suspended five feet off the bottom, and he dropped down to a reef chiseled low to the sea floor, and lay behind it, the speargun resting on its crest. He waited for the length of a breath-hold, but the pargo did not make an appearance, and wasn't seen on the ascent. His frustration begged the question; just how sensitive is this world? Does it pick up every little movement? Every sound? Does it feel my pulse? How can Messias make it look so easy. It's almost as if he were invisible to the fish.

Twenty yards from the last sighting several pargo laid in a narrow crevice of a reef. In a change of tactics, he dove straight down and pulled himself along the bottom using the rocks as handholds. Reaching the reef, and peeking over its edge the tips of dorsal fins could be seen waving at rest. Moving the speargun into position, he aimed at the nearest fish and pulled the trigger. The spear stuck the pargo near its midsection and it bolted out the open end of the crevice, into deeper water. The pargo was strong for its twenty pounds and it pulled McCorkin a dozen feet, before his strong kicks stalemated its rush. The pargo's resistance also prevented McCorkin from rising, and after fifteen seconds of furious kicking and needing a breath, he released the line. In an instant the fish darted into a cave on the forty foot bottom. On the surface, McCorkin pulled in the slack line and tied it off to the floating boat fender. Recapturing his breath, he floated above the entrance of the cave, marked by the protruding spear shaft.

Flushed with fresh air, he dove to the cave. Reaching the spear shaft he held it in his left hand and wiggled his right hand into the fish's gill. Then yanking on both the shaft and the fish, he wrenched the fish free. On the ascent the bleeding fish let loose the sharks that circled in the recesses of McCorkin's mind. Words of caution were remembered from Gonzaga: "If sharks are in the area they'll show up right after a fish has been speared." McCorkin did a quick three-sixty turn in mid-ascent, looking for dark shapes on the far edges of visibility, and tangled the trailing line around his right fin in the maneuver. Reaching the surface he unwrapped the line and scanned the water again, then swam for the anchored boat, two hundred yards to the northwest.

The weight of the thick-scaled, large-toothed pargo, whose dull beige color in the filtered depths had transformed in the surface light to a brilliant lobster red, registered on his forearm, conveying worth in its twenty pounds. McCorkin was ecstatic, his breaths were deep and his body hot from roiling blood. The water felt like air and he had the distinct sensation of flight.

Reaching the boat McCorkin climbed aboard and laid the pargo against the transom, where it was dwarfed by the grouper of Messias. After cutting the spear point from the fish, he stood and restrung the shooting line, looking as he did to the northwest for a sign of Hall and Scolari. A two-foot sea chop prevented a distant sighting, so he climbed to the cabin and surveyed the ocean again, squinting into the glare of the late afternoon sun. The churning water gave no clues, so turning to the south, out of the sun's glare, he looked for Messias. McCorkin had an idea where he might be, yet it was several minutes before he spotted a fin breaching the undulating sea.

Intrigued by the size of fish that might be found that far offshore, as well as the man making the dives, he reentered the water and headed in the direction of the arching fin. Frequently during the swim he stopped and kicked high out of the water in an effort to relocate Messias, but couldn't find him in the sea chop. Fifteen minutes of swimming had him in the general area, and again he kicked out of the water. By sheer luck he spotted Messias thirty yards due west on the crest of an up-swell, as he himself was on the peak of an up-swell. His position to Messias puzzled McCorkin. If anything, he thought, I should have been east of him. Maybe there's a current?

Messias was face down in the water when McCorkin arrived, kicking against the current, holding position above the reef. Lifting his head, he acknowledged McCorkin, who removed his snorkel and asked, "seen anything?" Messias nodded that he had, and returned his face to the water.

The top of the reef lay below, perhaps fifty feet or more, and its configuration faded into the blue haze of the depths.

McCorkin would have liked to have asked Messias how deep it was to the bottom, but it was clear he wasn't interested in small talk. Messias inhaled deeply and then dropped down. Strong kicks sent him into a steep glide; reaching the reef he soared right over its top, and disappeared into the haze below.

It defied a particular law of reason watching a man descend into the depths and out of sight like that, and it further confirmed just how far out of his league McCorkin really was. After an immeasurably long time, Messias reappeared along the outside of the reef lifting upwards toward the ceiling, his legs in long sweeping kicks, the stiff blades of the fins bent nearly double from the stress. Rounding off the dive he resumed breathing with the steady rhythm of one who had just completed a brisk walk. McCorkin watched him make two more dives, and with really nothing to see, and anxious to dive in water that was accessible, he turned to leave when a school of amberjack—what the Mexicans call pez fuerte (strong fish)—swam between him and the top of the reef. Gulping several quick breaths, he dove for a closer look. This was his first sighting of an amberjack, and, unlike the grouper, whose muscled bulk permitted short bursts of speed that could take it to the refuge of a cave in rocky terrain, the amberjack had a powerfully arranged forked tail and a bullet shaped body that enabled it to swim at high speed for long periods in the open ocean.

The amberjack were as curious as they were fearless, and moved closer to McCorkin who had suspended at twenty feet. The lead fish was far and away the largest in the school, and looked to be as big as the grouper Messias had landed earlier. Enticed by the nearness of the fish, McCorkin leveled the speargun at it head and tracked it with uncertainty.

The school circled at a crisp pace. The lead fish closed to within eight feet of the spear point. Filled with a mix of apprehension and anticipation McCorkin pulled the trigger. The spear shaft struck high, well past mid-body, hitting no vital areas. In the white light of an electrical flash the amberjack burst off toward the open ocean, the trailing line whipping by McCorkin and running straight behind the fish. McCorkin regained the surface and inhaled three breaths before the end of the one hundred and fifty feet of line buoyed by the boat fender, lodged behind his armpit. The impact nearly lifted him out of the water as the fish ran for the open ocean.

Messias had heard the release from McCorkin's speargun, and immediately ascended. When he reached the surface McCorkin was gone. Kicking high out of the water, he looked out to sea, saw nothing and looked inside toward the island. Seeing no sign he turned again to the sea. A snap sighting caught a black wet suit silhouetted against a sky beginning to gray with incoming clouds from the west.

McCorkin tried spreading his legs and throwing his fins out at an angle in an attempt to put drag on the amberjack. The yellow line was as tight as a bow string, and the fish gave no indication of slowing down. McCorkin had been swept into a battle for which he had no experience, no knowledge, and over which he had no control. The further from the island he was towed, the more frantic his efforts to turn the fish. Alternately, he pulled on the line and spread out his finned feet. No maneuver altered the amberjack's course. In ten minutes he had been towed a half mile from the deep reef.

McCorkin measured his swim to the island and considered leaving the fish and heading back. Perhaps they could find it later in the boat, he reasoned. No, leaving it would be weak. Nobody leaves their fish. I'll stay with it, at least for awhile longer. What if sharks come? Then I'll leave it, fast. How much longer can that fish keep swimming with a spear in its side?

The amberjack ran strong for another ten minutes. A change in tension on the line alerted McCorkin that it was weakening. He put as much drag on the line as arms and legs could muster. Gradually the line yielded, and with aching biceps, he began to haul up the fish. Eighty feet down the amberjack glowed silver/white against the depths. The tail, forked like a giant scythe, came into view, then the dorsal fin, raised in anger like a serrated knife. The fish was enormous, and it glistened of amber. Its head was larger than McCorkin's torso, and its black eye, as round as a coffee cup, darted from the hunter to the open water. He drew in the fish until it seemed to fill the ocean. Grasping the spear shaft, he slipped a hand into the space between the two gill openings under the mouth and squeezed. With the fish secured he lifted his head from the water and let loose a wild bellow of triumph.

McCorkin's joy was short-lived. He was well off the island now, perhaps a mile or more. Not an unswimmable distance, but more distressing was his position to the island. The current had pushed him east, almost beyond its southern tip. Gathering up the speargun, he wasted no time in heading back to Cerralvo. "Get as close as you can," he instructed himself; "they'll find you. Don't panic; that's the main thing. Just keep it together and stay alert for sharks." The word/thoughts rolled out, one on top of the other, forming a tape loop that played as he swam.

McCorkin swam for twenty minutes, pausing frequently to gauge his progress. Gain was imperceptible, and he picked up the pace, the tape loop running in sync with his kicks. Up ahead, a dark shape in the water brought him to a halt, and caused him to loosen his grip on the throat of the amberjack. Seeing that the shape was a man, he called to him, "Ray, is that you?" Messias swam to him, and in conspicuous relief McCorkin burst out, "Take a look at this fish, Ray! Can you believe it! Man, what a fight!"

Messias pulled the snorkel from his mouth. "We're in the mainstream current, Andy, we got a long swim. Stick close behind me," and he ducked back into the water and kicked for the island. McCorkin heaved a deep breath, releasing the tape loop with his exhale, and fell in behind Messias' wake.

The two bucked the quartering swells and wind chop that came out of the northwest, often taking water through their snorkel tubes. Messias snatched quick looks at the island, taking bearings and monitoring their progress. After thirty minutes of swimming, McCorkin's arm had cramped from the weight of the amberjack, and his legs had lost some of their snap. Gradually he fell off the pace and trailed a length behind Messias. Soon it was two lengths, then three, and he stopped and called. Messias halted and motioned him to catch up.

"My legs are starting to die on me. I'm having trouble staying up with you," gasped McCorkin.

Messias reached out his hand.

"Give me the fish, and stay inside my slipstream. It'll cut the chop and make the swim easier."

During the exchange McCorkin took a long look at the island. "We haven't gained on the island at all! We're being pushed beyond it!"

"We have to keep quartering off this current," replied Messias. "Once we get into the lee of the island, even if we're beyond the tip we should be able to swim up to it. Let's go."

Free from the weight and drag of the amberjack, McCorkin was able to maintain the pace. During the swim he realized that with or without the fish, it would have been doubtful he could have made this swim alone; his fear would have eaten up strength and left him floundering. Messias had saved his ass.

The swim progressed into its second hour. McCorkin's thighs were tight and losing power, and his ankles were turning to jelly. Messias steadily pulled away. McCorkin lost sight of his white water and stopped to call. Messias lifted his head and waited. McCorkin caught up, "I don't have much juice left in my legs."

"You're going to have to reach down and pull, Andy. It's a grind, but what's the alternative? We best take off our weight belts, and remove all but two four pounders.

"Why don't we just drop the weight belts?"

"We couldn't swim. The wet suit's too buoyant, our kicks would be out of the water. Might need the belts later."

"What for?"

"Who knows? Just keep it."

"How about the fish? Maybe we should dump it."

"No, we may need it later too."

"Why?"

"No more talking. We're losing ground." McCorkin unhooked the weights from his belt, and dropped them one at a time, leaving eight pounds on his belt which he recinched around his waist.

The fourteen pound weight loss made a difference, if not in McCorkin's swimming speed, then in the sensation of newly acquired strength. Confidence somewhat renewed, he busied himself in the details of the adventure, running it through his head for future telling.

The two sustained a steady kick. Messias continued to take bearings. There was a chance, he thought, if we can keep up this pace.

McCorkin stayed with Messias for a half hour, then began to wallow in the burgeoning seas. Repeatedly he glanced at the island to monitor headway. They were closer, but not close enough. The outlook of a short time ago faded along with his legs, and false confidence gave way to desperation. "Ray."

Messias heard the call, and waited.

McCorkin caught up, "I don't have anything left, Ray. You go for it. Give me the fish, and go for it. You could make it by yourself. Find Frank and Jeremy, then come back and pick me up."

"That idea had crossed my mind, Andy, but it'd be dark by the time I reached the island. Even if the boat picked one or the other of us up, it would be near impossible to locate the one still in the water. This wind chop and swell really cuts down our chances."

McCorkin lifted out of the water, doing a three-sixty turn.

"Where the hell is the boat anyway? Shouldn't they be looking for us?"

"They're looking. Jeremy and Frank won't give up on us. They've got an hour and then some before dark. Are you sure you can't go any further?"

"My legs are gone, Ray. I've sucked all I can out of them. What are we going to do?"

"We'll wait for Frank and Jeremy." Messias unsheathed his dive knife, and put it to the half submerged amberjack, running the blade along its back next to the dorsal fin, and down to its tail. Making an incision behind the bone next to the gill plate, he ran the point of the knife, just under the skin, down along the top of the belly to the tail. Another cut was made in the same fashion several inches below the original incision at the gill plate.

"What are you doing?"

"Making a flag. Here, open the gill plates," said Messias, who planted his finned feet against the wide open plates. Using the leverage, he pulled the skin of the amberjack down to the tail and cut it away.

"Hang this on the tip of your spear point, and hold the gun up in the air."

McCorkin pierced the skin and secured it with the two barbed point, then hoisted the silver and white flag six feet into the air. Looking up at it he declared, "They ought to be able to see this , no problem."

The overcast sky in the west obscured the setting sun. A thin, ashen line delineated the gray sky from the gray sea. Between swells and white caps the silver fish flag twisted in the wind.

Through the next half hour the two alternately rose out of the water on strong kicks at the top of the swells searching for the boat.

"Over there," said Messias, pointing to the southern tip of the island, which was now several miles northwest of their position. "The boat is halfway between us and the island on the outside. Wave the flag."

McCorkin waved the speargun.

On every up-swell Messias checked the progress of the boat. Jeremy and Frank were running a zig-zagging search pattern, and were heading in their direction, with a half hour of light left it would be close.

McCorkin's arms tired, and he exchanged spearguns with Messias. "Hey, I can hear the boat's engine under the water. Keep coming boys, keep coming," yelled McCorkin into the wind.

Methodically, the Pescadora worked her way closer.

In the fading light, the outline of the boat could be seen three hundred yards away. "Over here! Over here!" shouted McCorkin, "Goddam it, over here!"

Suddenly the Pescadora changed course, and sprinted out to sea.

"What are they doing?" McCorkin scarcely whispered the words, "What the fuck are they doing?"

"They probably spotted a bird or a seal or something. They'll be back."

"It's getting too dark; they'll never find us now." McCorkin's words came out in a whine, and sounded far away and unfamiliar to him.

"Take it easy, Andy," said Messias evenly. "If they don't find us tonight, then we spend the night in the water, and they pick us up tomorrow." McCorkin, stunned into silence looked into the darkening depths; adrift on the open ocean at night was the one thought he had managed to avoid.

Messias lowered the fish skin flag, knowing that Jeremy and Frank couldn't see it unless they came to within fifty yards. Both men, each in their separate worlds, listened to the sound of the boat's engine, until its whine diminished with the last light.

❖ 3 ❖

"IT'S GONNA GET DARK FAST," said Messias. "We better fillet out the amberjack, and dump the carcass before the sharks sniff it out. Take the weights off your belt and stuff them inside your wet suit, behind your ass. That should keep your legs low in the water so you can swim. We'll use the belts to secure the two boat fenders together, and lay the fish on top. We won't need the poly line; we could try wrapping it around our chests and stomachs. The insulation might keep us warmer. Clear the cable from your poly line and hook it through the belts on the floats. Just let it hang in the water for the time being."

"Won't we need the shooting line in case of sharks?" asked McCorkin.

"If they come, the last thing we want to do is give up our spear shafts. We might need them later to spear fish. Only as a last resort do you want to pull off on a shark. We can defend ourselves by jabbing them with uncocked spearguns."

McCorkin's mind spun in anxious circles. "How big a search party can Jeremy and Frank raise?"

"The Americans will come, however many there are, but the Mexicans will probably want to be paid. It'll be easier for them to believe that the sharks have already done the job."

"What are you saying?" McCorkin's voice was frayed. "You think there's a chance they won't come? Or there won't be enough boats or something?"

"They'll have plenty of boats," said Messias reassuringly. "But we've got to assume that it might take awhile, so move your weights, unhook the line, and secure the floats. While you're doing that, I'll fillet out fish strips. You hungry?"

"I haven't thought about food."

They removed the weights and stuffed them down their backsides, then lashed the fenders together with the weight belts, making a two-by-one foot float, and heaved the amberjack atop it. McCorkin steadied it while Messias cut inch-wide strips of meat a foot long from one side of the fish and draped them across McCorkin's outstretched arm. When he had cut away five pounds Messias punctured the air bladder and sent the carcass to the depths. The strips were laid across the float, crisscross fashion so they wouldn't slip into the water. "The evening sea dew will settle on the top pieces, and we can eat those for breakfast," said Messias. "While we're at it, we best hook ourselves to the fish float so we don't get separated during the night. Take the end of that cable hanging from the floats and run it through a couple of strands of poly line around your body. Make it snug so it will hold, but where you can pull it out if you need to get free."

They connected themselves to the fish float, and Messias lifted a strip of meat from atop the stack and rolled to his back. The sweet, fresh taste of the raw fish cleansed his salty mouth, and dissolved easily in soft bites. "Andy, try this amberjack, it's delicious," he said, tearing off another bite.

McCorkin looked at the meat, sighed, and lifted a strip. Following Messias's lead, he turned to his back and gnawed off a piece. The first bit resurrected his lost hunger, and he devoured the strip in progressively larger mouthfuls nodding in sync with his chewing. "Hey, this ain't bad."

Between swallows, Messias told McCorkin, "During the Arctic winters the Eskimos existed for who knows how many centuries, eating nothing but raw fish and raw seal meat, six months out of every year. How long do you think you could survive on raw fish, Andy?"

"As long as I had to, Ray. As long as I had to." For emphasis he ripped off another chunk and chewed it with resolve.

They each finished three strips and floated in silence. Behind a thin seamed cloud cover a piece of opalescent moon rose out of the swells in the east.

McCorkin broke the quietude, "What kind of sharks are out here, Ray? I bet they get pretty big in this open water."

The casualness of McCorkin's remark belied his dread, and Messias responded to the obvious. "Don't think about sharks, Andy. They're like hypersensitive dogs. They smell fear, the dying and the dead. You start running sharks through your head, and the fear builds up until that's all there is. You wind up a freaked out bundle of nerves, and the sharks home right in on that."

"But what'll we do if they come? What's the plan?"

"If one or two come sniffing around we'll unhook from the cable and chase them off with a few good stabs from our spear points. If more come, or they start to get twitchy, then we'll go back to front. I'll cover your back and everything to my right. Are you right handed?"

"Yeah."

"Then you do the same. Cover my backside and everything to the right."

"Jesus, I hope to Christ..."

"Don't think about it," interrupted Messias who knew that McCorkin was already filled with sharks, and would think of little else through the night. "Because sharks are a possibility," he continued, "we'll have to take regular underwater watches. One diver keeping an eye on things, while the other floats and rests as best he can. I'll take the first watch."

"No, Ray, I'll do it. There's no way I can relax. You stay where you are. I'll watch."

"Okay, call me in an hour for relief. If something comes up, give a holler."

Messias stayed on his back, laying the long gun down the center of his body, and rested his head on the edge of the fish float. Seams in the overcast sky had parted slightly, and stars jitterbugged in and out of the cracks. He tried to find Venus among the narrow faults.

McCorkin turned and floated face down in the water staring into a galaxy of another kind. Nothing, he thought, could be so black as the open ocean at night. Yet, within the blackness, there sparkled the same white light of the stars; glittery phosphorescence abounded.

Every movement of his head created sparks of silver light. They careened about his face like swarming fire flies. Luminescence trailed from his speargun as dust from a sorcerer's wand. Were he in the shallow waters of a shore line, he might have enjoyed the magical display. As it was, it only seemed to accentuate the infinite blackness above which he dangled.

"Hey Ray, I can't see anything. A shark could be right on top of me before I could defend myself."

"You'll see it in the phosphorescence," answered Messias without lifting his head from the fish float. "The movement will give it away. You'll have plenty of time if one shows. It'll come in easy and work its way to the surface. Don't think about it."

McCorkin tried to clear his mind. Already his imagination was conjuring images out of the black water. He strained to see beyond the twinkling light. A feeling of utter exposure pervaded him, as though he were shining like a midnight sun above an alien world of invisible creatures.

The ocean and his imagination conspired to unravel him. Its movement upset his stomach. And his eyes, in their relentless search, found nothing stationary on which to rest. Distant shapes formed in luminescent whirlings and dissolved. The internal commands of relaxation and deep breathing were suffocated by a choking anxiety. McCorkin's tension grew, and his right forearm began to cramp from the fierce grip he had on the speargun.

A force was felt. It seemed to rise from the depths and pull at him from the belly. It reduced him, and he felt small and weak. He had encountered the surface power of the ocean enough times; its storms, its waves, its undertow and currents; but never this. It's my nerves, he thought. My imagination is making this happen. Yet there was a realness to it that could not be denied. It was unremitting, like a black hole in a faraway universe, sucking to its core all that was loose. Early on he convinced himself that the sensation was a manufactured one, but as the hour wore on he knew it to be real and it frightened him.

The tension in McCorkin's body forged it ridged. The rise and fall of the swells turned his stomach, and he became dizzy and nauseous.

Unable to roll with the ocean, or contain his anxiety, or settle his stomach, McCorkin threw up. He heaved up the amberjack, his tension and his fear, again and again. Messias left the fish float and came to him.

"You okay, Andy? You got anything left to puke before we go?"

McCorkin was on his back, and lifted the face mask to his forehead. He looked at a piece of moon with watery eyes. "I'm okay. Why do we have to leave?"

"The puke will draw sharks; stay on your back, and hold on to the cable. I'll tow us away from here."

"You don't have to tow me Ray, I'll be all right." Messias towed the fish float east, going with the swells. The pace was easy and McCorkin followed behind, watching the phosphorescence stirred by the action of Messias's fin movement. It felt good to be swimming, to be doing something other than floating, and staring into nothing. The movement brought a temporary warmth, and steadied his revolving head. They swam a considerable distance before stopping. "This should be enough," said Messias. "You take it easy and I'll take the watch." McCorkin drifted to the fish float. The cloud cover continued to break up and clusters of stars collected across the sky. "Keep your eyes to the moon and stars," advised Messias, "and the motion won't bother you as much. Try and find Orion and Sirius. Over to the left and above your head is Venus."

The moon and stars conveyed a permanence and McCorkin's troubled mind found comfort in them. His father had often taken him camping when he was a boy and he remembered how pleasant it was to sit in the glow of the campfire, protected from the darkness and all that it held outside its circle of light. Resting in his father's arms he would look out into the night, and freely imagine every sort of creature lurking in the shadows, knowing no harm would come to him. McCorkin's thoughts wandered to his childhood, seeking sanctuary in its past pleasures.

Messias's voice came from afar and penetrated McCorkin's cushioned dreams. "How are you doing, Andy?"

McCorkin's head slid from the fish float, sea water washing over his unmasked face. "What's up Ray? Is everything all right?"

"Everything's fine. It's been a couple of hours, and I'm beginning to feel a little woozy myself. Can you take the watch for awhile?"

"Yeah, sure. I must have dozed off. What time is it?"

"I've no idea, maybe around midnight."

Six more hours before dawn, thought McCorkin, shaking from the cold. Rinsing the taste of bile from his mouth, he reset his face mask and turned to the ocean, its abyssal blackness extinguishing what remained of his inner campfire.

Vaporous shadows at once besiege him, leaving the way clear for the sharks to navigate back into the hemispheres of his brain. He fought the images, and tried to think of Cynthia, but the sharks consumed every thought, devoured each fantasy until they thoroughly possessed him. Straining to see beyond the blackness, he twisted and turned to cover exposed flanks and rear, never seeing anything, but never sure he was seeing nothing.

McCorkin's mind was descending into recesses as black as the water, his madness looming in the twinkling phosphorescence. Afraid of completely losing his grip, he struck a fantasy to detour the debilitating slide. If I could be anywhere right now, he thought, it would be with Cynthia; lying in her bed, having her warm body curled into mine, stroking her, listening to her breathing…The fantasy was obliterated by a phosphorescent movement below. He looked at it, unwilling to believe it was actually there. He couldn't speak until the sight of a triangle fin released his voice, "Ray, there's a shark below."

Messias slipped the gun from his chest and eased away from the fish float. He rinsed out the face mask, secured it in a single motion, and dropped his head into the water. A nine-footer was weaving a pattern of light twenty feet beneath them.

McCorkin's fear oozed from his pores. He was helpless to either stop the shark, or control his terror of it.

The tapered body of the shark left stardust trailers in the nigrescent water. Messias had encountered sharks before and was familiar with their body language. This one appeared to be scavenging, looking for the easy meal, and shouldn't pose a threat. Still, one could never be sure.

The shark ascended in an unbroken figure eight pattern, and came to within six feet from the surface. When it swam directly beneath the divers Messias dropped down and thrust his spear point into the top of its head. The shark wheeled violently at the impact, and burst off the spear in a flurry of phosphorescence. A rocket gone awry, it flashed brilliantly, then disappeared into deep ocean space.

The two laid on the surface watching for luminescent indicators. None appeared and Messias lifted his head from the water. "Nothing to it. They're all chickenshits."

McCorkin smiled a weak, unconvinced smile. Messias asked if he wanted to rest for awhile. McCorkin refused, saying that his watch was not up. Then, feeling his cold and hunger, recanted, "Yeah, I'd like to try and eat something. I'll come back when I'm finished."

He went to the float and eased a fish strip from out of the middle of the stack and bit off a piece. The shark wasn't so terrible, he thought, not like I had imagined. Sucking and chewing on the raw fish, he relived the encounter in his mind. Each time he played it, his tension lessened and his fear found passage through his breaths. Taking the experience a step further, he imagined himself diving down, thrusting the spear point into the shark's head, and watching it bolt away. Resting easier than he had all night, McCorkin finished the fish strip.

The sky was nearly cloudless. A three-quarter moon reflected brightly off the black sea. The swells elongated the moon's reflections on the up side, and compressed them on the back side, so they appeared to be passing through a time warp. McCorkin had the distinct feeling that his presence here was a mistake. Unaccountably, he had been cast into an ordeal that was not his to endure. So disturbing was this revelation that he forced it from his mind and thought instead of Cynthia. They had made love once on a beach under such a moon. Afterwards they had watched its scattered reflection on the water, and talked of the future. Death was not a part of it. Death lay beyond the future, an event that existed in a lifetime yet to come. But this night he had seen the face of death and in a strange way felt more alive for having seen it. Messias's voice came from behind the fish float, "Andy, you ready for a turn?"

"Yeah." McCorkin settled his face mask over his nose, and rolled to his stomach. A spasm that could have come from the cold, rippled through his body. No, he thought, looking into the starry depths, you know there is time. Don't lose it, breathe easy, stay relaxed.

Despite the words, despite the knowledge that was gained from the recent encounter, despite all that he could do, the fear crept in. It was not the paralyzing fear of the helpless victim; the unknown, at least in part was known. It was a fear born of vulnerability that caused McCorkin's head to swivel and all thoughts of Cynthia and the outside world to be absorbed by the blackness of the ocean, as the color black absorbs the colors of the spectrum.

The swells rolled under him, and their movement worked his stomach as before. Numbness reclaimed his limbs, and he asked the sea, "How many more hours before daylight?"

The sea spoke its sounds, but it did not speak of hours, or of daylight. Its language was unfamiliar and fell uncomprehended.

"I am nothing in this ocean," said McCorkin to the sea sounds. "I am so insignificant you don't even know I exist." Thoughts that had never been granted entry into his consciousness were slipping through cracks that had been opened by the nearness of death. To the sea sounds he continued, "Man is weak. He just goes through the motions of power, the bullying, to keep from seeing his weakness, his death. Everyone is scared shitless all the time. No one knows what the hell is really going on. They're all afraid."

A flowering phosphorescence stopped his thoughts cold. Then another glowing shape materialized, and another, and another. "Ray, sharks, at least four."

Messias released himself from the cable that connected him to the fish float. Bringing his face mask down, he left the last trace of a moon that had dipped into the west.

McCorkin's breaths came in short, chopping blasts. Of the four sharks, now five, one in particular was much larger than the others. Tapping Messias on the shoulder, McCorkin lifted his head from the water and spoke rapidly, "What're we going to do? What if more come? Should we go back to back?"

In an unwavering voice Messias replied, "This is nothing we can't handle. As long as they're moving slowly, we can punch each one away when it comes into range. If more come, or they start to get twitchy, we'll go back to back. Take what's in front of you and to your right. I'll do the same. Don't over commit yourself; let them come to you."

The sharks tracked their way to the surface in figure eight patterns. McCorkin counted seven in all; his heart pounding like a signal drum, pointing the way. He moved closer to Messias, almost touching him. The sharks swam nonstop. Several cut behind them, and Messias turned to cover their exposed backside.

The largest shark swam out of the pack, and cruised eight feet beneath McCorkin. Bending at the waist, his upper body dropping two feet below the surface, he drove the spear point hard into the top of its head. The creature lurched, then whipped away, nearly wrenching the speargun from McCorkin's grip. Jolted by the thought of losing the gun, he fastened both hands to it and shakily resurfaced. McCorkin's peripheries caught Messias's fins lifting as his upper body bent into the water. An instant later a burst of phosphorescence ignited the water as the speared shark thundered off into the void. As another cruised closely by McCorkin leaned down, and with both hands on the speargun stabbed it hard in the head. It thrashed off in a shower of sparkling light.

The sharks rose in serpentined waves and each took a piece of McCorkin's mind when he had speared it. Soon all thought ceased and his mind became a blank screen. His eyes scanned the water and reported their findings to the blank screen. The range and speed were calculated and the body was deployed with faultless precision. McCorkin was responding in absolute fearlessness, and had no awareness of it.

The two men held their ground, driving off each shark as it came into range. The water frothed with silver light. The blank screen in McCorkin's head anticipated which shark would move into him, and he would wait and time his strike for the effective blow. It became a discipline; waiting, waiting, holding off until the shark was no more than a yard stick away, then thrusting down, using the body and arms to drive the spear to its target.

At the moment preceding each strike the shark became clearly visible, as if a light had been switched on. McCorkin saw its snout, eye, gills, dorsal fin and tail. He also saw that not all the sharks made passes; only the large one and three others were the aggressors. The rest circled below waiting for first blood.

The large shark twitched and turned, and after several preliminary passes, it came in a rush, making straight for McCorkin. He'd been watching it, waiting for it, sure it would come, and met it with a bold thrust when it was five feet away, hitting it squarely on the nose. It bucked and twisted at the impact. The water swirled beneath him as the shark burst away, scattering the sharks below, and breaking up the macabre dance of light.

In that single moment the battle that reached its climax, and fell to absolute stillness. Messias turned and floated head to head with McCorkin. They waited. Minutes passed. McCorkin lifted his head from the water. "You think they'll come back?"

"Who knows?"

In the starlight, McCorkin's broad grin gave him a boyish look. "We did it Ray! Did you see that big one, coming in at the end! It must have been twelve feet long. Man, I hit that sucker right in the nose."

"You did real good, Andy."

"What kinds of sharks were they?"

"Gray ones," said Messias, smiling.

"No, I mean the species."

"Duskies maybe. Does it matter?"

"No, I guess not. I can't believe this night." Rotating in the water McCorkin looked at the sky. "How soon before dawn? Which way is east?"

Messias pointed across McCorkin's ear, "Over there."

"How can you tell?"

"The swell has been coming from the northwest, unless it changed while we were busy with the sharks. We're a couple of hours away from dawn."

"Why don't you kick back Ray? I'll finish up the watch."

"You got it, Andy." Messias swam back to the fish float and hooked himself up. The man knows no fear, thought McCorkin. It's like he's done this before, and knows exactly what's going to happen, and what to do about it. When we were trying to make that swim to the island, he could have left me in the water and gone for it himself. He would have made it. I'm going to throw him one hell of a party when we get back, spend every cent I got.

The adrenaline producing warmth brought on by the shark attack burnt away, and McCorkin's body temperature dropped to a chilling low. The cold replaced the sharks as a major point of concern, and he drifted toward dawn, shaking in icy purgatory.

McCorkin figured that the sunrise was at least an hour away, yet he lifted his head every few minutes, looking for subtle changes in the sky. Eventually, a color change began to occur. Distant starts fell, and the pale blue precursor of warmth signaled the end of his longest night.

The phosphorescence, which he had come to rely on to detect movement below, also began to fade with the incoming light. Generally, in the daylight the visibility in this open ocean was in excess of two hundred feet. At the moment the water was an opaque blue, and the visibility appeared to be no more than twenty feet. The change was disconcerting because the unseen now lay but a few feet away. Dark, amoebic shapes appeared, some as large as a car and they undulated ten feet below the surface. They came and went, seeming to stay just beyond sharp visibility. In distrust of his eyes, McCorkin tried to blink them away, as if they were a mirage. But they remained, and more shapes appeared, some smaller, some of equal size. Whatever they were, the ocean, as he thought he understood it, had acquired another mysterious dimension. Was it possible that in this vast and unknown expanse, other worlds were housed; worlds that only revealed themselves in those moments before the sun rises? McCorkin was uneasy. Not afraid as he was with the sharks, but spooked like a dog when it wanders into unfamiliar woods that hold strange and foreign odors. The blanching sky closed the visibility down further, and the dark demons roamed nearer. In an untainted wilderness such as the open ocean, he concluded, anything was possible; the demons were real. The rational side of him fought such a speculation, insisting that these images were a product of hallucination, that nothing so obvious could exist here in the late twentieth century without the knowledge of man. Yet, there they were, dark and fluid and pulsating. The eye providing irrefutable proof. The rational mind and its cohort, logic, had been on shaky ground these last hours, and could not sustain the argument. McCorkin remained unswayed. It would have been a comfort to have had a second opinion, and he considered asking Messias, but was afraid to speak up, fearing that if they didn't exist, Messias would think he was cracking up. Which might be too near the truth to risk the asking.

Messias called from the fish float, "Andy, how about some breakfast. We best eat the fish and whatever sea dew has collected before the sun breaks the horizon."

McCorkin went to the float, and they each took a fish strip from the top of the pile. They floated on their backs and quietly ate the first strip. Reaching for a second strip, McCorkin said, "There were a couple of times last night when I had my doubts about being around for breakfast this morning."

"Well, you're here, so the fish ought to taste especially good." Messias smiled and took another bite.

In three thousand feet of water, with no land in sight, the two dined on the amberjack, carefully picking pieces of fish from a one-by-two foot table that floated south of the Sea of Cortez, where it emptied into the Pacific Ocean.

❖ 4 ❖

THE MEXICAN SKY WHEELED FROM OCHER to pumpkin to freshly minted gold. McCorkin couldn't remember a more beautiful sunrise. As the sun's first tendrils pierced the surface, he ducked into the water; the demons of dawn had vanished. Driven, no doubt, to the far reaches of their grotto by the light. The steep angled rays turned the water a cobalt blue that appeared infinitely transparent. The wind meandered in whispers, and the swells, no longer deep troughed, as they were closer to land, stretched out evenly, diminishing the sensation of rising and falling. McCorkin rose out of the water on strong kicks. "Where the hell are we?"

"Hard to say," said Messias looking at the sky. "There's no way to gage the speed of the current we're in. If its held to five or six knots, then we might be fifty or sixty miles from Cerralvo."

"Fifty or sixty miles! How many boats at the marina have that kind of range? That's a hundred and fifty miles round trip, plus searching all day. Shit, we'll be lucky if a half dozen boats can come this far."

"Well, they should have a fair idea how far we've come. The Mexican fisherman know the currents out here. I don't know if we've picked up another current coming down out of the gulf, or if we're still in the same one, or if we've hit a dead spot. There's no way of measuring our drift. The one thing we do know is that Frank and Jeremy will have a full twelve hours of daylight to find us. By sundown we'll be back drinking beer at the cantina telling this story to the whole town." McCorkin's face crinkled into a smile. Messias had been right so far, and his doubts, like the sea demons of dawn, withdrew in the light of hope.

They laid on their backs, sunning themselves in slow liquid turns, the sun delivering its coveted warmth to their quaking bodies. After a time Messias broke the quietude with an unexpected announcement, "We've got to hunt for another fish."

"Another fish?" McCorkin was puzzled. "Why do we need another fish if we're going to be drinking beer at the cantina this afternoon?"

"We've got to assume that we might not be found today. The sun is warming us now, but it'll be a bitch in a couple of hours. A real thirst is going to build and fish is our only source of liquid. Besides, it'll give us something to do."

"What kind of fish swim out here? It's like an underwater desert. How the hell are we going to find fish?"

"More likely the fish will find us; dorado, wahoo, sail fish, tuna and marlin run in these water. We'd have trouble with marlin, large tuna and sailfish. They're a high risk fish. They'd probably take us and our rigging to the far ends of the Pacific. Sharks run with tuna schools. We might be asking for trouble if we tied into a tuna. Our best chances are with the dorado and wahoo."

"Isn't the water too deep? Couldn't they just sound and take our rigging right out of sight?" replied McCorkin in half-hearted argument.

"If we splice our lines together, that would give us three hundred feet. We don't need the cable out here. There aren't any rocks to cut the line, we could secure the line directly to the buoys. A good shot might slow one down enough. We could work the line together, create drag, make it work for every foot. You'd have to stay on the surface and handle the poly line. Keep your gun ready if sharks come, or we need to second shoot the fish."

McCorkin grinned wildly, "Whatever you say, boss."

"I'll have to dive without a wet suit top," said Messias. "We don't have enough weights for a full suited dive."

"How much weight you going to need?"

"We got enough. Using your eight pounds, plus my eight, should be plenty with the farmer johns. You ready to go to work?"

They uncoiled the poly line from around their bodies. Messias spliced the two ends together and refastened one end to his spear, and wrapped four lengths of shooting line the length of the gun. He removed his wet suit top and handed it to McCorkin. "Better tie a line through the sleeves and lash it to your wrist. I don't want it lost in the heat of the chase. I'd have a rough time making it through a night without a full wet suit. Make sure the line is long enough so you can hoist the wet suit up on the speargun for a hailing flag. If we got separated in the chase, it'd be the only way we'd have of connecting up again."

"This amberjack is going to spoil as the day wears on," continued Messias. "Take a half dozen strips and slide them inside your wet suit. They'll stay a little cooler there as we float along, and a thin layer of salt water won't hurt either." McCorkin worked the pieces of fish inside his suit, and Messias removed his weight belt from the bound floats. They extracted the lead weights from behind their legs and Messias strung them to the belt. After hooking it around his waist he dropped down to a neutral buoyancy depth of twenty feet and hung motionless. Returning to the surface he declared the weights to be acceptable for the dives he had in mind.

The brilliantly clear water gave McCorkin the impression he was floating in air. Turning himself over to the sensation, the tug of the depths that was felt last night, again pulled on his gut. So strong was its presence that he was surprised he hadn't recognized it sooner. He reconsidered the demons of dawn with new perspective.

The speargun was rigged and cocked. Messias dropped down, the yellow poly line marking his descent. McCorkin was struck by the fragility of the man, hanging there so vulnerable in that wall-less blue glade. Close to shore, or off an island, man had shown a capacity to survive, an ability to function with a certain degree of effectiveness. This open water was a different wilderness. Here, there were forces that overwhelmed man, even a Raymond Messias. Although these forces could not be readily identified, they clearly existed, and had frightening power. It seemed merely a matter of time before the ocean would absorb them both into its tissues, as it had done to tens of thousands of ships and men since man had put to sea. The two of them were living a precarious existence, one that couldn't go on for very much longer. It was a miracle they lasted the night, it would be another to make it through the day.

It didn't seem physically possible that Messias could actually spear a fish, thought McCorkin. Where did one look for a fish in this water—up? Down? Straight on? Behind? A fish could come from any direction, if it came at all. Messias suspended in the water like a man waiting in the middle of an open desert with a rifle at the ready, expecting game to suddenly, magically, appear. Although McCorkin believed it was an exercise in futility, he nevertheless took pleasure in watching Messias make those fluid, boundless, breath-hold dives of his. So enraptured was he, that Messias once swam to where he floated and reminded him to keep an eye on the horizon for boats. He also suggested caution with the rising sun, saying it would be wise to take off the wet suit and top and drape it over his head for added protection. The warmth of the sun was delicious after the frigid night, but he'd begun to feel its heat, so removed the top and covered his head. If, in the unlikely event Messias did spear a fish, he could easily slip an arm through the hood hole, and not lose the top in the chase. The water temperature was nearly seventy degrees and in the morning sun the farmer johns were pleasantly comfortable.

Mid-morning, and neither man had seen a fish, nor a boat, nor a plane. Messias had stopped making dives and was watching for fish from the surface. Both felt the pangs of thirst, and each took a fish strip from McCorkin's wet suit, dipped it into the sea water and ate it wordlessly. When finished they resumed their underwater watch, McCorkin regularly checking the horizons for boats and planes.

The morning passed without a sighting, either above or below the water. The sun was near its peak, and McCorkin was about to suggest they eat another fish strip when, materializing out of the empty blue, a silver marlin glided into view. From the tip of a three-foot long bill to its grand furcated tail, it was as stunning a creature as McCorkin had ever seen. The fish seemed to radiate in an incandescent light of its own making. It coasted along without any apparent tail or fin action, and passed directly beneath them at a depth of twenty-five feet. Messias dropped down, as though he had intentions of spearing it. Against such a fish he looked hopelessly overmatched, and the moment he cleared the surface the marlin accelerated its glide. Reaching neutral buoyancy, Messias hung motionless and the fish continued its flight, doing a half turn before disappearing behind translucent shafts of filtered light. Messias floated up to the surface and McCorkin greeted him.

"You weren't actually thinking about spearing that marlin?"

"It did occur to me."

"We couldn't stop a fish like that. What if the shot was a shade high or low. It would've taken everything!"

"At this point we have to take the chance."

"Jesus, Ray, I don't know."

"The sighting could be an indication that more are in the area," instructed Messias. "Keep a sharp eye. If another comes along, and I drop down, secure the wet suits and get ready for a ride."

Spearing a marlin was dangerous and foolhardy, thought McCorkin. If it were anyone else, he would have argued in favor of waiting for something smaller to come along. He had complete confidence in Messias, and would do anything he asked—but a marlin?

Messias nudged McCorkin's arm. Three marlin, swimming in formation, cruised below. McCorkin's heart ran to his throat, and he unconsciously readjusted his grip on the poly line. The marlin moved with a restrained power that accentuated their stately presence.

That Messias could actually bring one down seemed inconceivable.

He made his drop. McCorkin ran an arm through the opened zippered front and out the hood hole of the wet suit, and rechecked Messias's top, making sure it was secured to the poly line.

Messias glided toward the marlin, trying to quarter off the leader, which was larger than the one seen earlier. The three fish faded off their course, putting distance between themselves and the intruder. Messias stopped at a depth of twenty feet and swam in the opposite direction. A yellowtail trick that will often pique a pelagic's curiosity. The marlin were either too wise or disinterested, for they did not flinch from their course. Messias waited until they had swam from sight before returning to the surface. During his ascent two more marlin swam into view. Out of breath, and unable to pursue them, he and McCorkin watched them glide regally on their way and out of sight. "This looks like the motherload of marlin," said McCorkin through his snorkel tube.

By the time Messias had regained his breath the water was empty of fish. They waited, anticipating another sighting. McCorkin's eyes jumped about the depths in the quick movements of a bird of prey.

Twenty minutes passed before they saw marlin again. Three emerged out of the blue, seventy-five feet away, at a depth of thirty feet. Probably the same three we saw awhile ago, thought McCorkin. Messias exhaled and inhaled, and dropped down. The marlin altered course, sliding away from his drop point. Rather than trying to cut them off he hung in the water slightly above their depth level. The marlin maintained their course. From the opposite direction came a single sailfish. McCorkin held his breath. This fish was coming close enough for a possible shot. Messias swung the speargun to line up on the sailfish. At it's nearest point he pulled the trigger. The spear shaft hit high, well behind the gill plate. The sailfish accelerated for the depths with such force that the trailing line, which ran to the surface, whipped up and caught Messias' arm, very nearly wrenching the speargun from his hand. McCorkin squeezed the flying line and tore open the palm of his thick glove. Both men converged on the line, trying to get a grip on it. Messias had slipped his arm through the slings of his speargun, freeing up both hands and managed to get a hold of the line, and was instantly pulled under. McCorkin wrapped an arm over the line in time to hook the floats as they zipped by and was also pulled under along with the speargun and the two wet suit tops. The combined drag of the two men discouraged the sailfish's initial run, and it made a deep turn, heading back in the direction it had come. The line slacked, and they released it and swam for the surface. The sailfish was too deep to see, but a long loop in the yellow line indicated its turn. Under heavy breaths, they hauled up line that had slacked with the resurfaced floats. Twenty feet was retrieved before the deep loop began to straighten. McCorkin took a hand hold in front of the floats, behind Messias. They scarcely had time to inhale a breath before being yanked down. Dropping at a forty-five degree angle to the surface, the speed of descent was such that the force of the rushing water broke loose the seal of McCorkin's face mask, and while holding the line with one hand, he used the other to push the mask, half filled with water, back into place, and kept it there to equalize the rapid pressure changes. In fifteen seconds, and at a depth well beyond his limit, he released the line. The additional buoyancy of the two wet suit tops probably saved him from drowning. He reached the surface with head reeling and body tingling from oxygen depletion. Keeping his face to the water, he gulped breaths through the snorkel, and watched, horror stricken, as Messias was reduced to a black dot in the depths. Silently he pleaded, "Let it go Ray, let the goddam thing go." The dot that was Messias enlarged with his pleas. He was ascending, the speargun looped around a shoulder, his hands empty.

Messias reached the surface thoroughly spent, and rolled to his back, heaving in great lung-fulls of air. Between breaths, he said, "It was tiring there at the end."

"Take it easy Ray, get your breath back, we gave it a shot. There's no way we could find it now. It could be anywhere. It's probably laying somewhere in eight hundred feet of water waiting to die."

Messias pounded out his breaths, and didn't offer a response. Sensing what might be coming, McCorkin continued his passive argument. "It didn't seem possible from the beginning. We never really had a chance with the fish. You'd almost have to make the perfect shot, and hit the backbone."

Messias, who had regained his breath and was treading water, gestured for an exchange of spearguns, and McCorkin did so without dissent. "Stick close. Keep your eyes sharp for the white floats. You look left and I'll look right." And he swam off in the direction the sailfish was last heading.

Messias swam in a southerly direction for two hundred yards, then inexplicably changed to an easterly direction. McCorkin stayed close to his side, and they swam for a half hour. Certain that the search was a waste of time, McCorkin grew weary of the endless blue and his concentration waned.

Abruptly, Messias changed direction again, swimming southeast now, and stayed to that course for a quarter of an hour. Something caught McCorkin's eye enough to jar him from stupor. Looking again, below and to the left, a white blemish appeared in an otherwise perfect sapphire. Jabbing Messias, he pointed down in near disbelief for it seemed impossible that such a small thing could actually be found in this expanse of blue. It was as if Messias knew precisely in which direction to swim.

Messias stopped and they treaded water. "It looks like the fish is still on."

"How can you tell?"

"If it had gotten off, or was hit by sharks, the floats would have risen. I think the fish is spent, and resting deep. I'm going to try and bring it up." He handed McCorkin his speargun, and lay directly above the floats, which were suspended in what McCorkin guessed to be about a hundred feet of water. Hyperventilating much longer than usual, Messias drew in one last breath and bent into the water, dropping down vertically, a black pearl descending into a glycerine sea. He reached the floats that were well beyond McCorkin's hundred foot guess, then turned for the surface. Behind hard kicks he rose at a slow and agaonizing pace.

In a minute he had come half way. McCorkin could see he was laboring. Gaining another twenty feet, Messias looked up and motioned McCorkin down. McCorkin quickly secured the wet suits to the speargun and left them floating, pumped up six deep breaths and dove. Without weights he had to kick to neutral buoyancy. Once past twenty-five feet, he was able to glide the short distance to Messias, who shoved the line in his hand, and shot for the surface. The fish was astonishingly heavy and McCorkin sank from its weight. Kicking frantically, he halted his descent, suspended for a moment, then slowly began to rise. The effort was an immediate drain of strength and oxygen. Pressing upward, he didn't look above his head to measure the distance to the surface for fear it would steal his breath. Fifteen feet from the top he was completely out of breath, his legs tingled and brilliant flashes of light bounced around the inside of his skull. He considered letting go of the fish, but knew if he did it would drop like a stone and be lost for good. Bearing down he made one last, desperate push. In the next moment he was floating on his back, breathing comfortably, and Messias was speaking.

"Andy, you all right?"

"Sure Ray, I feel fine. Where's the fish?"

"I have the line right here. You blacked out five feet from the top. Your arms and legs shot straight out and the line slipped from your hand. I dropped down and caught it and pulled you to the top."

"How long have I been out?"

"About a minute. How're you feeling?"

"I feel fresh. I'm okay. That's weird. I passed out? I felt something coming on. It was getting short there at the end. I thought I could make it."

"Well, you did the job."

"I don't know how you got as far as you did, Ray. That fish weighs a ton!"

"Yeah, it stretched me. It was a mother all right, but the weight comes from all the water above it." Messias flipped to his back and rested with McCorkin.

McCorkin couldn't quite believe that the sailfish was actually on the line. "Well, something is weighting it down," said Messias. "If you're ready, let's haul it up, and see what it is."

"Yeah, right," said McCorkin, "seeing is believing."

"Keep the floating line down current and away from you," cautioned Messias. "If the fish makes another run, you don't want line looping around an arm or a leg. It could take you down for keeps. You better cock your speargun. We might have to second shoot it. You've got a free shaft in there, so make sure you hit the fish or the shaft is history."

They began hauling up the line, their surface buoyancy making the job easier. At a hundred and fifty feet the fish's outline was visible. A flash of reflected light glanced off its side at eighty feet. "Here she comes," said McCorkin. Forty feet from the surface the sailfish glowed an iridescent blue the length of its streamlined body. The three-foot bill was as long as the forked tail was wide. Its majestic head and large eyes couldn't belong to any but the noblest of ocean predators. The sailfish's radiant beauty was highlighted by a spectacularly large dorsal fin, for which the fish was named, and flared atop its back like a grand mantilla. Similar to eminent creatures of the land, there was an essence to the sailfish which lifted it above its ocean brethren and into that rarified air where soared the magnificent works of nature. McCorkin was mesmerized by its stunning grandeur.

The sailfish bolted weakly when it neared the surface, pulling Messias down two fathoms before stopping. Resurfacing with the line in his hand, he said, "I don't think we ought to mess with this fish until it dies. We'll double loop a long line around its tail, and secure it to the floats. It'd be better to keep it cool and alive in the water for as long as we can anyway. At least until the sun starts to drop. It's not bleeding much. If sharks haven't shown by now, they probably wont. Still, we should keep an eye out." Messias secured the tail, and McCorkin asked how much he thought the fish weighed.

"It's as large as a marlin, probably around a hundred and fifty pounds."

"Man, I still can't believe you did it."

"We did it. Now all that's left is to have a boat show up."

"Yeah," said McCorkin, "cause no one's going to believe this unless they see it for themselves." Messias's reference to the boat brought McCorkin back to the core of their predicament, and he kicked out of the water, searching the horizons in a three-sixty turn. An afternoon wind was developing, bringing with it a sea chop. The sun reflected harshly across the broad expanse of jumping water, and McCorkin squinted into it. An object appeared in the distance that didn't fit into the surface picture he had been observing since dawn; a white bowed sail coming out of the south, on a starboard tack, the wind off its port beam. "Ray, a sail boat!" McCorkin pointed to the southern horizon.

Messias rose out of the water on an up-swell and saw the boat. "Yeah, she's coming our way. If she holds to that tack, there's a chance they might spot us.

For the next twenty minutes McCorkin repeatedly kicked up out of the water, and enthusiastically reported the boat's progress. Messias kept an eye on the sailfish and the surrounding waters for sharks that were curiously absent.

The boat had sailed to within a mile of them, and McCorkin raised the speargun with Messias's wet suit attached, and steadily waved it back and forth. He had trouble watching the boat and waving the flag, and had to drop it for a better look. The sailboat appeared to veer slightly from its course, pointing higher into the wind, prompting McCorkin to suggest that they swim after it.

"We couldn't make much progress swimming into this building chop, towing the fish," Messias advised.

"Maybe I should take out after it. This could be our only chance."

"It's up to you, but if you miss it, we probably won't be able to connect up again."

McCorkin searched out the boat again to further weigh his chances. During their brief conversation, it had changed course, and was on a port tack. "They're moving away from us," moaned McCorkin, who continued to watch the boat for a few moments longer. Then he stopped kicking and sunk back, the speargun/flag slipping from his hand. He dropped his face into the water to hide his anguish and Messias swam to him and patted him on the shoulder. McCorkin kept his face in the water, his breaths echoing through the snorkel tube in choking exhales.

The sun leaned heavily on the western horizon. Messias watched the water for sharks leaving McCorkin to himself.

Inside an hour the sailfish died.

Messias pulled it up, and with McCorkin's help slipped the floats beneath it. The weight of the fish was more than the floats could support, and it sank several feet below the water line. Messias cut a large chunk of meat out of the neck and divided it, offering half to McCorkin. The sweet, firm meat scarcely drew saliva from their mouths. They ate without speaking, and when finished, Messias said, "The sun is low enough, we may as well start butchering the fish."

The neck, above and behind the gill, was cut down to the backbone. "When we're through," said Messias, working on the incision, "this will become our permanent flag pole. We'll stand the head of the fish on the floats, tie it down with poly line and hang the skin from the tip of the bill. It oughta stand up about five feet out of the water." From the deep incision at the neck he cut parallel behind the gill plate, and with the point of the knife split the skin along the top of the back and down the belly the fish's full length. "We better saw off these long dorsal spines before we strip the skin. We might be able to use them later on. You have saw teeth on your knife, Andy?"

McCorkin nodded that he had.

"All right, you start aft, and I'll work from the head down."

"Why are we doing all this bullshit," blurted McCorkin suddenly. "So there's some memorial for a boat that might pass by in a couple of months?"

"Andy, our job is to stay alive," Messias replied calmly. "We've got to do everything we can to keep going until we're found. Jeremy and Frank won't give up on us, and neither can you. Now let's get to work." McCorkin shoved the snorkel in his mouth and bit down, the glare of the sun on his mask obscuring the despair that had permeated his eyes.

They sawed away on the dorsal spines, the task requiring concentrated effort in the rolling seas. After the spines were cut away Messias straddled the fish, placing a finned foot against an opened gill plate for leverage, and pulled the silver/blue skin down its five-foot length. "This is going to make one hell of a flag," he said, piercing the skin with the fish's bill.

"Andy, while I fillet out this side of the fish, you work your knife between the spinal cord at the neck where I made that deep cut, and sever the head from the body."

Messias, who had seen the mares tails on the southern horizon some time ago, looked up from the filleting job. "There could be a storm brewing. Mares tails are beginning to shape up in the southern sky."

"Maybe we'll get some rain," said McCorkin, tying his hope to the wispy clouds.

"Maybe." Messias glanced back at the sky.

McCorkin sawed through the spinal column, until the head with attached gills separated from the body. Both men strained to lift it to the floats. McCorkin held it erect while Messias ran a line up and across the fish's mouth and down to the floats then up through the eyes and back down through the eyelets on either end of the floats. The five-foot long fish skin flag drug in the water, and he cut a foot off its end so that it freely curled in the wind. They placed the long dorsal spines in the fish's mouth and eye sockets, which gave it a wild, demonic look. "You think this'll keep the sharks away at night?" asked McCorkin, smiling again.

The talisman grew to bizarre proportions when they impaled strips of fish meat on the naked spines. "More likely it'll turn away sensible boaters," laughed Messias. With all spines filled to capacity, two thirds of the edible meat remained on the sailfish.

"We should eat as much as we can now," advised Messias, handing a five-pound chunk of meat to McCorkin. "We'll have to deep six the fish before it gets dark."

McCorkin held the meat in one hand, hefting its weight.

"I can't eat all of this."

"Eat all you can. It's not going to get any fresher." Messias cut a piece for himself, then punctured the air bladder of the beheaded fish and sent the carcass to the depths.

McCorkin watched it make a lazy, spiraling descent to the blue underworld. In the ultra-clear water it appeared to suspend, but he knew it was sinking. He could feel the pull of the fathoms on his stomach, and spread his legs and arms wide and clung to the thin veil of the surface. Lifting his face from the water he joined Messias, who was floating on his back, pulling flesh from a chunk of meat that was resting, sea otter style, on his stomach. Together they studied the mares tails in the azure sky. Midway through their meal McCorkin said, "I think it's pretty amazing that I'm stuck out here with probably the greatest spearfisherman than ever lived. I mean yesterday you didn't even know me from a grouper, and today here we are... It's weird."

Messias shook his head in discomfort with his notoriety.

"Come on, Ray. You oughta hear the way everyone talks about you. You're a legend."

"Hardly," answered Messias shaking his head again.

"How long have you been diving, anyway?" asked McCorkin, heedless of Messias' discomfort.

Messias looked up past McCorkin as if he was looking for something on the far horizon.

"Long time," he finally said.

"Was that before or after swim fins were invented?"

Messias burst out laughing with such genuine infection that it turned McCorkin's grin into open laughter.

"After," replied Messias. "But not too long after. Somewhere between swim fins and wetsuits."

"You've seen alot."

Messias nodded in slow, distant agreement. His laughter fading into reverie.

"It must have been sometime back in the sixties," continued McCorkin. "Were you from, California?"

"No, Bellingham Washington. I didn't move to California until I was sixteen years old. Started hitting the kelp beds from Laguna to La Jolla in the early sixties." Messias paused for a long moment. "The ocean was my hiding place. My second home."

"So where was you first home?"

A veil of constraint fell across Messias' face and thickened his voice.

"I left it when I came to California."

Oblivious to Messias' reticence, McCorkin pursued with enthusiasm. "I've never stuck with anything for very long. Got too bored, you know? What locked you into the ocean for all these years?"

Messias took a breath and released it, lifting the veil of his refuge.

"By the time I was in my late teens, I had a pretty good feel for the ocean. There was something inside of me that understood it.

I felt connected to it in a way I've never been able to explain. Some people can pick up a guitar and play it. I walk into the ocean, and it plays me. I learned more about the world from the ocean than from any school, but it was stuff no one really cared about."

"What sort of things did you learn?"

Messias paused a long time before answering. "Important things, like how to see, really see something. Not just give it a glance and define it, but see it in a larger picture. See the connections. The ocean showed me how things tied into one another. You know what I mean?"

"I'm not sure," said McCorkin, who hadn't a notion of what he was talking about.

Messias knew he hadn't understood. "Awhile back I was at a Christmas party of a friend of mine. We had worked together as carpenters and done some diving. Anyway, he liked to hang out with professors from the local university, and there was a mix of them at the party. I wandered from group to group, eavesdropping on their comings and goings. Some marine biologists were all very excited over the completion of some three-year project. They had discovered a bacteria, found in the upper intestinal tract of Pacific sea lions that was killing them. The odd thing was that it was a bacteria produced exclusively in the sea lion's lower intestine. There was no physical way it could work back into the upper tract. It had been a real mystery to them. I thought I knew the answer. They were ready to have some fun with me, and insisted on an explanation. I said that as far as I knew the opaleye were the only fish that eats dung. If a sea lion craps around an opaleye, it'll gobble it up in a flash. A healthy sea lion really doesn't like to eat opaleye, but if it's lazy or sick, it'll eat one because they're easy to hit. If it happens to eat one that has just eaten sea lion dung, then the bacteria will get back into the upper intestinal tract."

"Was that right?"

"Yeah, it was right. Anyone who has spent time around the ocean knows about the opaleye. Yet these college guys had to spend three years, and who knows how many thousands of dollars to figure it out. They had no sense of connections. The obvious had become a major mystery to them, and in the end so what? Sea lions and opaleye have been doing that forever. It's academic masturbation, something they do to justify their salaries."

"I bet they shit when you told them," grinned McCorkin.

"I don't remember." Messias paused. "It's connections, Andy. If you start to see the connections things begin to make sense. Sometimes you can feel it all tie in together: the ocean, the inhabitants, you, everything." Messias looked into McCorkin's face for a sign of comprehension.

McCorkin misinterpreted it as an invitation to another question. "What did you learn from spearing fish?"

Messias released an audible sigh, "We got off the track here, where were we?"

"I don't remember. All I know is that I'd be dead right now if it wasn't for you. I appreciate you putting up with my bullshit."

"It's not bullshit, Andy. We're in a tough situation. It doesn't do any good to get down. It just eats up energy. We'll pull through. We have to take it hour by hour. A boat will come."

McCorkin nibbled on the chunk of sailfish until he was full, then flipped it into the water. He turned over and watched it sink, a disconnected pendulum swaying in the crystal water. Completely exhausted, he surrendered to the motion of the jumbled swells.

Messias remained on his back, pulling apart the meat with his fingers, pondering the southern sky. If a storm does come up, he thought, they'll call off the search until it blows over. If we're not found by sunset today, then its going to be at least two more days adrift. Without water we're going to have a rough time. I doubt we can last much longer than that. If it does rain, we're going to have to find a way to catch the water and store it.

"Ray! Ray! My speargun is gone! I was floating in the water. I had it in my hands, then it was gone!"

Messias put his face to the water and saw nothing. "You must have dozed off and dropped it," he said, treading water again.

"I'm dead without a speargun," wailed McCorkin.

The loss of the speargun was critical to the survival of both men. We have so little to work with as it is, thought Messias, to lose anything is disastrous—to lose a speargun...

McCorkin was in a fitful rage, talking aloud to himself. "I can't believe it! I might as well drown myself now and be done with it." The sharks of last night swept before him, and he envisioned himself pushing them off with bare hands. "It'll just be a matter of time before I'll be bitten. There's no fucking way."

"Take it easy, Andy. I'll take the spear shaft out of my gun, and you can use it as a prod. It should work as well as a speargun. I'll lash my knife to the muzzle of my spear stock."

The idea made sense to McCorkin, and the boiling sharks in his brain settled beneath the surface. "I feel so stupid Ray, so incompetent."

"Don't get down on yourself, Andy. It could have happened to me."

"It would've never happened to you, Ray."

"Just the same, we've got to take extra precautions now. Our judgment is going to be affected by lack of sleep, thirst and fatigue. We'll have to keep a close eye on each other. You best tie a couple of lines around your arm, so you can slip the shaft under them. If you fall asleep again, there won't be any chance of losing it."

McCorkin cocked his head to one side, "You hear it?" Lifting out of the water he spun around, and stopped facing south. "A boat!"

Messias kicked out of the water. A half mile southwest riding atop a following sea, plunged a Mexican trawler with green gunwales. McCorkin whistled and shouted and frantically waved his arms. The trawler stayed to its course, plugging along in a southeasterly direction. "Do you think they can see the flag?"

Messias, intent on the progress of the trawler, did not answer. It looked like the same shark boat that yesterday had leveled the rifle on him. Was it only yesterday? It seemed a week ago. There was something strange, almost foreboding about that boat, thought Messias. "They're not running a search pattern. They're hunting sharks. Probably going to lay down long lines before dark. All hands are below sleeping, and the helmsman is probably half asleep himself."

McCorkin shouted after the plodding trawler until he was hoarse. Slamming his fist into the water, he said, "The only way we'll ever be found is if we are run down by a boat and jam up the prop."

"The sharkers are a good sign and a bad sign," said Messias. "We could see more boat traffic out here, but it's possible that there are more sharks in this area, which is why the Mexicans are here in the first place."

"Swell," said McCorkin, lifting empty hands into the air.

"We won't be doing any spearfishing for awhile," said Messias. "Go ahead and take the spear shaft. I don't have to tell you where we'll be if you drop it." Pulling the trigger, Messias released the shaft from its housing. Untying the poly line from the slide ring, he gave the spear to McCorkin. Craddling the stainless arrow in the palm of his large hand, McCorkin squeezed it shut finding a firm grip difficult on the thin barrelled shaft. Still, he thought, slipping it under the two lines tied around his forearm, it's better than nothing at all.

Messias cut a three-foot length of poly line, and laid on his back with the speargun stock held between his legs. Placing his dive knife under the muzzle in the same fashion a bayonet is fixed to a rifle, he tied the line over the muzzle and around the handle of the knife so the spear shaft could be reinserted and the rubber tubing pulled back into cocking position without having to re-move the knife.

McCorkin lifted his head from the water as Messias finished the job. "Ray," he fairly whispered the words, "an enormous shark below us." Directly beneath them drifted an oceanic shark of mammoth proportions. It was by far the largest Messias had ever seen in the water; twenty feet long, with pectoral fins that ex-tended three feet out on either side of its four-foot wide body. A school of yellow and black pilot fish hovered about its blunt nose, and a large remora clung to the back of its head, well in front of its massive dorsal fin.

McCorkin swam to Messias as the shark made its turn and came back toward them. This was the kind of shark McCorkin had seen in films, taken from the safety of a shark cage. Those films didn't begin to capture the awesome power that this shark exuded. The thin metal spear shaft in his hand felt puny and worthless. McCorkin's heart pounded and pressured his lungs. Adrenalin released into his body for flight, but there was nowhere to flee. The fighter, in face of the overwhelming adversary, froze in paralysis upon the surface.

Messias dropped down and aggressively swam toward the shark, trying to bluff it into retreat. The shark faced him straight on, unmoving, forcing Messias to stop dead in the water. At a distance of fifteen feet, they stared each other down. McCorkin, in his disabled state, could only watch the scene unfold. Neither the shark nor the man yielded. Overmatched by some forty-five million years, Messias was finally forced to rise for a breath. In the ascent the shark cruised beneath him, turning its black eye to his swinging legs.

Messias reached the surface and was met by McCorkin, who sought reassurance by way of a quick glance. It did not come. Messias' face was grim; he did not take the creature lightly.

Messias wanted the shaft back in his speargun. There was no protection against a shark of this size. An arm powered thrust of a spear wouldn't faze it. Only a fully cocked, well placed spear shaft might have a chance of turning it. McCorkin's lost speargun was already taking its toll. Strange, he thought, that despite the spearing of the sailfish, and all the commotion that raised, no sharks appeared. Yet when that white and green trawler turns up, so does this shark.

McCorkin lifted his head from the water, and spat out his snorkel. "What are we doing to do?"

Messias shrugged. "Watch it and wait. We've got no choice." The two floated in crossing swells. Every so often a crest of a wave lifted them above the plane of the ocean and a southerly wind blew across their backs.

The shark lay ten feet down and circled counter-clockwise thirty feet away. McCorkin's anxiety ridden mind filled itself; what is this shark waiting for? What will we do when night comes? Is it sensing my fear? Will it come for me first? McCorkin's fear was compressing him; breaths were restricted. The became dizzy and his body went numb.

The stand-off went into its second hour. McCorkin's fear had pinched out the past and the future, and Messias had became a distant fragment drifting on the edge of his peripheries. The ocean existed only where it housed the shark. Soon the shark itself became blurred, and McCorkin saw his own reflection in its black eye. Cogent thought had abandoned its sanctuary of reason, and his mind, unanchored, floated toward oblivion.

The impasse continued as the sun fell to the horizon. McCorkin's body had detached from the peril and lay suspended somewhere above the surface. There remained for him but two courses; either complete acceptance of his impending death, or catatonic sleep, to which he was already dangerously close.

As a balloon bursts when filled beyond capacity, so did McCorkin burst from his swollen anxiety. Surrendering to his death, he accepted in its totality all that it implied.

Under the terms of such a surrender one is instantly transported to another country—that of the dying. A place where time and space in their respective elasticities have stretched to such thinness that in their transparencies they cease to exist in the way the living recognize them. McCorkin's body resumed its place in the water; his breathing returned to normal. His vision regained its clarity and his head cleared itself of accumulated cobwebs. Blissfully empty, he perceived the shark in a different light. It had transformed from an object of his terror to a creature of elegant line and symmetry, possessing a restrained power similar to that of the sailfish. The shark carried itself with timeless immortality and McCorkin observed with sober esteem, the oldest, unchanged creature on the planet.

The shark drew McCorkin into its ancientness, delivering him back to its prehistoric time. The layers of his acculturation peeled away, leaving him naked and cleansed to his primordial bones. He floated in this boundless state, free of any fear of death.

The low sun turned the water smokey and the shark glowed silver, and appeared to enlarge. As in dream change, there came a bright flash of movement. Something had come and gone before McCorkin could interpret what it was, or what had happened.

Messias saw it all. Three dolphin had come blazing in at high speed. One hit the shark at mid-body with its forehead, and the other two struck behind the first assault. The shark, along with the dolphin then evaporated onto the graying water.

"What happened?"

"A miracle," said Messias softly. "Three dolphin came in and hit the shark solid in its mid-section, and drove it off."

"Everything will be all right," assured McCorkin with uncharacteristic calm. "They knew we needed help."

"I don't know," answered Messias. "Strange things happen in the ocean; most of it is an absolute mystery. I couldn't begin to try and figure it out."

"The dolphins understood." McCorkin said it with such confidence that it caused Messias to look directly into his face mask. "They'll protect us," added McCorkin.

Messias waited for further explanation.

When it didn't come he said, "Maybe, but I wouldn't want that shark to come back to test your theory. We best eat something before it gets dark." He pulled two strips of meat from a fish spine, and handed one to McCorkin.

They ate supper floating on their backs exchanging little in the way of conversation. Messias observed that McCorkin had made a dramatic change. There was an air of confidence about him. He appeared thoroughly at ease and self-assured. Well, thought Messias, this kind of experience was bound to change a person, one way or the other. He could have easily gone the other way.

The sunset was spectacular. McCorkin had seen his share of sunsets, but this one he perceived like no other. Acutely aware of every hue in color and light, he allowed its transformations to pass unobstructed by preference, and accepted the earthly gift as though it were created for him alone.

An ebony sky overtook and absorbed the last light, and Messias, having seen the rapture in McCorkin's face, hooked him to the fish float, saying, "Stay where you are Andy. I'll take the first watch."

McCorkin had lost himself in the first evening stars, and Messias' earthly words fell faint and far away. The night sky soon glowed liked luminescent sand on a black beach. Wide-eyed, McCorkin knew not of his predicament. All was in perfect order. Later the moon, like an alabaster scallop, rose out of the swells in the east, and mingled with the sparkling sand. The moon aroused thoughts of Cynthia. They were not the thoughts of the terrified man who last night longed to be safely in her arms, but reflected the depth and beauty of the woman whom, he realized, he truly loved. On this night ocean he saw the moon's benign glow to be the same light which back-lit her soft brown eyes, and gave them their warmth. Love had replaced longing, and McCorkin knew he would spend the rest of his days with Cynthia.

Messias interrupted McCorkin's reverie with a nudge. "How about relieving me for awhile, Andy?"

"Sure Ray," and he slipped his head from the fish float.

The carbon waters McCorkin faced this night were of another sea than those of the previous night. The phosphorescence no longer accentuated the profound depths, nor did it disorient his eye. It twinkled in a show of boundless energy, weaving patterns of light into the muddied abyss. Floating loose and easy on the surface, McCorkin smiled in recognition of this effervescent world which had laid before him last night and was not so perceived. It inspired him to wonder what other universes danced before his eyes, yet remained unseen. There came the revelation that he was observing, perhaps for the first time, his surroundings as they might truly exist. This discovery brought with it the understanding that Messias observed the ocean with this same unobstructed clarity. How would it be, he thought, to experience daily life with these perceptions—to see this clearly without the barriers of fear to cloud the mind. It would change everything! When I return to the civilized world, will I fall back on old habits? Will old fears dominate me? Will I forget what it is to truly see? Forget how wonderful the dances of light? Forget that they are forever whirling in celebration, whether I can see them or not?

McCorkin thought he heard it before he saw it. Like rolling thunder it came, vibrating with phosphorescence fifty feet away at a forty degree angle from the surface. The shark was enormous, as big as the one this afternoon, and it moved quickly.

Lifting his head, he calmly announced, "Ray, big shark below." He returned his face to the water as the shark accelerated toward him with jaws agape, and scarcely had time to point the spear before it struck. The spear shaft sank into the cartilage inside the mouth of the lower jaw. The impact forced McCorkin's right hand down the thin shaft and into the shark's mouth, and pushed his body up and off to the left of the creature, which had turned at the bite of the steel. The shark closed its mouth around the shaft as McCorkin pulled his hand away, painlessly opening up his wrist, nicking an artery.

Blood was pouring from the wound when Messias arrived. McCorkin, in control of his faculties, handed the spear shaft to Messias, then pulled the wet suit open at the sleeve and squeezed his forearm above the wound in an effort to stop the flow of blood.

Messias jammed the slightly bent spear shaft into the trigger mechanism of the speargun, quickly cocked one band and was reaching for another when the shark, with incredible swiftness, came again. It headed straight for McCorkin and the blood. Inserting his finger into the pistol grip, Messias pulled the trigger of the already raised gun, firing it point black into the swirling phosphorescence. The shark's momentum carried it into McCorkin, the spear shaft whipping his arm with a glancing blow as the shark turned at the impact of the spear hitting the side of its head.

The only sounds were of sharp breaths through snorkel tubes, and the sea slipping off itself.

"How bad is it, Andy?"

McCorkin held the arm up to the moonlight. The wound was four inches long, running three inches across the wrist and an inch into the meat of the hand below the thumb. Despite his attempt to check the flow of blood, it spilled from his wrist at an alarming rate. "It doesn't feel too bad. It throbs, but there's not much pain."

Messias removed one of the rubber slings from the muzzle of the speargun and tied a tourniquet around McCorkin's forearm, stopping the blood flow. "Float on your back, Andy. Take it easy, you lost some blood. I'll keep an eye on things in the water."

"Yeah, I'm feeling a little shakey now."

Messias checked the water again. There was no sign of the shark. "I think it's gone. We'll be all right. You rest."

McCorkin stared at the moon.

With the fish float and McCorkin in tow, Messias kicked away from the blood spoor. He had swam a half mile before stopping at McCorkin's call. "I'm feeling cold Ray." McCorkin was shaking and his breathing came shallow and quick. "I'm really thirsty."

Messias felt his pulse. It was rapid and feathery. He is going into shock, thought Messias. A wound like that could be taken care of on land, but out here, without fresh water for a day and a half, cold and exhausted. . . His thoughts trailed off. "Just take it easy Andy. Hang on. We'll be out of this by tomorrow morning."

McCorkin stared unblinking into a moon that had risen directly above them.

"Cynthia."

"Who is Cynthia, Andy?" McCorkin didn't answer. Messias turned on his back and floated beside him.

Several times McCorkin spoke unintelligible words, as if he were having a conversation. "What, I can't hear you?"

Three dolphin broke water fifty yards away.

"You got here too late," whispered Messias.

"Who's talking?" said McCorkin.

"It's okay, Andy. I'm right here. Stay with me, kid."

McCorkin began to struggle for his breaths.

Messias put an arm beneath his shoulders and lifted him slightly to ease his labor. As he did, McCorkin heaved in a deep, gasping breath, released it and stopped breathing.

No attempt was made to revive him. There was nothing Messias could do. Reaching over with thumb and forefinger, he closed McCorkin's eyes.

❖ 5 ❖

ATTENDED BY THE THREE DOLPHIN, Messias stayed with McCorkin's body through the night. Glad for the dolphin's company, he relaxed the shark vigil and dozed. Waking, he would roll over, peer into the phosphorescent ocean, turn again to the sky and moon, listen for the sounds of the dolphin's exhales and fall asleep again.

Near dawn he awoke to violent shivering. A foul, bitter taste lay on his tongue and he lifted the top strip of sailfish meat from the fish float and licked its surface moisture. Replacing it, he selected another that held promise of sea dew. Six pieces were taken and together they scarcely invited a swallow. Floating on his back, he ate the last piece and gazed into a somber sky. It would be dangerous for me to assume that I'll be found, Messias thought. The odds against that possibility increase with every hour that passes. Survival is in my hands. I'll need water, food, and must somehow find a way to stay out of the ocean during the night or the exposure will kill me as surely as any shark.

Taking inventory of his goods, he tallied three hundred feet of poly line, two rubber boat fenders, McCorkin's pair of swim fins and his own, two face masks, two snorkels, two dive knives, two weight belts, sixteen pounds of lead weight in four pound increments, a speargun without a spear shaft, three twenty-eight inch long 9/16" rubber tubing with accompanying wishbones, two ten-foot lengths of stainless cable, two sets of neoprene booties, two sets of gloves, a sailfish head with attached gills, eight sailfish dorsal spines ranging in length from two to three feet, and enough meat, that, if not exposed to the sun, might last another day.

He finished the fish strip and the inventory at the same time and took a second strip. The still hidden sun ignited the high flying mares tails into tangerine streamers; the long branched clouds turning icicle white at their uppermost tips. On the horizon, gray cumulus tumbled northward. The storm will reach me sometime around noon, he thought. In that time, I've got to find a way to catch rain, and store it. A gentle nudge of McCorkin's body returned him to an undone task.

"I could be envying you in a couple of days," he said to the body of McCorkin. "For you it was quick and painless." Removing McCorkin's fins, booties and face mask, he secured them to the fish float. Then stripped off the wet suit top and farmer johns, leaving McCorkin naked save for his swim suit.

It would have benefited Messias to have left McCorkin's body floating on the surface. There was always the possibility that it might be found, and thus extend the search for him in the general area, but that was not considered. For the scavengers of both sky and sea, in collaboration with the sun and salt water, would soon mutilate the body. Tying one of the four pound weights to the pull string of McCorkin's trunks, he swam the body down and released it when it began to sink of its own accord. Without glancing back, he returned to the surface and the fish float, hooked himself up, and swam for the rising sun. The swim warmed him and his shaking stopped. The physical exertion also provided a release from the presence of McCorkin that had stirred in his chest through the night.

The wind out of the south had increased and the prevailing northwest swell was being overrun by a southerly chop that indicated grander seas to come. Gleaming thunderheads mushroomed in the distance, and Messias surmised that the storm might be upon him sooner than expected.

The sailfish flag, having stiffened during the night, laid like a silver/blue lame awning to one side of the fish's head. The skin resembled not so much an awning as it did a sail, and with a slight adjustment or two, a suitable rain catcher.

However, the skin of a dead fish was not the ideal material to capture fresh water spilling from the skies, and Messias replaced it with McCorkin's wet suit top, which he turned upside down, piercing the beaver-tail flap to the bill of the fish. Two dorsal spines were inserted and wedged between the breast and back to open the suit and keep as much area to the sky as possible. The result closely resembling an inverted, overweight, scarecrow. He lashed the muzzle of the speargun loosely to the base of the fish float, and raised it to the extended wet suit, lashing it at the neck so it slanted at a forty-five degree angle to the sky. As it was arranged, the rain would strike the opened suit, run down and collect in the well of the hood, and from there could be poured into holding containers. The matter of the holding containers would easily be resolved if at least one of the four neoprene booties was water tight. Messias filled McCorkin's bootie with sea water, closed off the opened end, and squeezed down. One bootie leaked at a seam, the other was water tight. He removed his own booties, and performed the same test, with the same results; one leaked, and one held water. Switching booties, he put the leaky one of McCorkin's on, and so had two sealed containers ready for rain. Unsure if two booties would be enough, and knowing it would be prudent to have an extra container rather than come up short, he cut the leg, from ankle to calf, out of McCorkin's farmer johns and tied it off at the ankle with a strand of the three part poly line. Three, foot long strands were also cut and stuffed down each of the opened containers. These to be used for tie-offs when the booties held rain water. The rough water hampered his efforts and more time was expended than anticipated.

Gray curtains of rain tracked northward, and dark undersides of the billowing thunderheads loomed five miles to the south. The southerly was blowing white water off the tops of broaching swells. There would be no search party on this ocean today, surmised Messias.

The storm was moving quickly, and Messias, west of the rain bearing front runners, would miss their fall. He swam easterly, kicking against the chop, attempting to intercept the main body of the storm before it passed, but the wind regularly caught the rain catcher, and forced it northward, inhibiting progress. He tried pushing the float and discovered that when turned to a particular angle the catcher acted as a sail and pulled the float along. So using his body as both a keel and rudder, he was able to improve headway.

The tropical bore down. To the east, a half mile distant, it was raining torrents. To the south, a black cloud dumped its cargo. The space between sky and sea were ashen with sheets of falling rain. Although at times it was surrounded by rain, the catcher remained as dry as a house cat. The storm sped northward as beams of sunlight seeped through broken sky, announcing the front's departure. It had come and gone in twenty minutes. Following closely on its tail, a secondary front blew off the near horizon.

Messias, who had spent the better part of his life on and under the ocean and had seen all it could offer a man in both hardship and beauty had long accepted its capricious ways. If nothing was presented, no gift extended, that was simply the way of things. This attitude didn't mean he was powerless, or imply a willingness to submit. It was, if nothing else, a call for resourcefulness. So treading water there in the white capped seas, and in obvious need of a boat, he visualized the construction of one.

The speargun was already attached to the fish float, and with McCorkin's farmer john wet suit rolled up into the shape of a sleeping bag and lashed to the free end of the speargun, it would lift the entire stock out of the water by six inches. A keel would be necessary to prevent the boat from slipping sideways on a beam reach. One might be made by placing a four pound weight into the foot space of McCorkin's two swim fins, and lashing them just above the instep to the wooden stock of the speargun, midway between the fore and aft floats. The sailfish spines, equally spaced and lashed under the wooden stock, could form the ribs of the boat, and the skin of the sailfish might do well as a center hull covering.

The rudder and tiller presented problems. The forked tail of the sailfish would have made a perfect rudder and tiller had he the foresight to keep it. What was needed was an elbow or bend, and there was only one such bend available; where the rear extension of the speargun met at a ninety degree angle with the pistol grip. Removing the extension would shorten the boat by a foot and a half, but there was no other choice.

The extended squall sent new thunderheads in on the secondary front as Messias set to work. He rolled up McCorkin's farmer john and bound it with two lengths of poly line, then removed the three spines of fish meat and laid them on top of the rolled wet suit which was steadied at its base by two, three-foot long dorsal spines. With the spines of fish strips laid aside, he was able to work on the sail.

The two spines that held the wet suit open performed much the same function as spreaders of a mast, and needed only to be secured to the bill of the sailfish. He ran poly line stays from the top of the bill to each end of the spreaders where they would later be secured to the forward float. The pistol grip, with attached extension, was unscrewed with the point of a knife, leaving the four foot long stock as his keelson plank. He lashed the rolled up farmer john to the aft end of the stock completing the floation for the boat. Next he ran a line from the top of the bill to the aft end of the stock as an aft stay, which strengthened the craft by forming a singularly contained unit in the shape of a triangle. He wedged a four pound weight into the foot space of each of McCorkin's swim fins, and pulled their heel straps over the stock and lashed them with poly line midway between the fore and aft floats to create a fin keel. The meat was removed from the fish spines and placed in the container cut from the leg of McCorkin's wet suit. The spines were then lashed perpendicular to and along the lenght of the stock. The fish skin, having softened in the water, was laid smooth and tight under the forward float, and tied beneath the spines as a center hull covering. One of Messias's swim fins was fastened to the end of the pistol grip, which finished the rudder, and a series of loops were woven around the rudder/tiller so that it was secure to the aft float, yet could be easily rotated. In this way, the boat was steered with the helmsman on his back and his feet resting on the aft buoy operating the tiller between bent legs. The last swim fin was lashed to the stock for a seat and Messias climbed aboard for a sea trial. The weight of his body lowered the boat several inches, and the heavy chop awashed him in sea water. The angle of the tiller was awkward and difficult to steer, and the boat refused to stay on an even keel. It continually tipped from side to side, eventually dumping him overboard.

Although much of his body had been submerged, and the sun had not been out in full force, Messias was entering his second day without fresh water. If not in the early stages of dehydration, then certainly he teetered on its edge and his thirst had him glancing to the skies. A mile southwest a gray film of rain descended from a charcoaled bottom cloud. When this front passed his opportunities would reduce to the thin line of broken clouds that trailed to the horizon. Unless the craft's flaws were quickly corrected, he might well be left with no opportunities at all.

The tiller was relashed to the aft buoy so that it tilted at an angle that better suited his upraised legs. Reluctantly, he removed his wetsuit bottom, rolled and tied it, as he did with the aft float, and secured it between number two and number three ribs, thus outrigging the starboard side of the boat. Lastly, the spreader stays were loosened so the sail could be trimmed to the wind.

Settling back in the center of the craft, with sea spray blowing across exposed legs, Messias maneuvered the sail using the spreader lines, trimming it as best he could for a starboard tack.

The outrigger provided the needed stability, and the weighted fin keel was more than adequate on a beam reach, keeping sideways slippage to a minimum. Reclining several inches above the water line he pointed east toward the western coastline of Mexico.

Sailing for a rendezvous point with a lone rain bearing cloud, he misjudged its speed and watched it pass a quarter mile east, dispersing rain drops which the wind carried close enough to spit disdainfully on the black sail.

The rear echelon of the storm dashed northward, and Messias continued to sail east, attempting to line up with another full bellied cloud. Once in its path, he removed the wet suit top and tied it across the spreader lines in front of the sail and, using the last fishspine, canopied the bottom of the suit at a forty-five degree angle to the sky and made ready the fresh water containers.

The gray canvassed cumulus loosened its weight upon the catcher. The shower fell for the length of the passing cloud, leaving nearly two cups of water in the hollow of the hood. Knees resting on the forward floats, and holding the aft stay for balance, Messias lowered his head to the hood and sipped in several mouth fulls. Adding a ration of sea water he drank another swallow, then poured what remained into an empty bootie and strung it to the aft stay where it could be watched for leakage, and be handy for showers yet to come. Still on his knees, he licked both the sail and catcher of droplets that clung to their surfaces. Then releasing the canopied catcher, he trimmed the sail for further pursuit of thunderheads.

Messias sailed into the sweet spot of the storm where trailing clouds regularly passed overhead. Few held rain, and fewer still let loose their payload. In two hours a cup and a half of water had been accumulated. To that, half as much sea water was added to the take of fresh. The combined cache came to less than three cups of drinkable water. Of that, he consumed half, and ate a rain washed fish strip. The faint odor of putrification foretold the last of the fresh fish. What was left would have to be dried to jerky. He ate two more strips, and chased them with another swallow of water.

On the hard edge of the southerly, the remnants of the storm slipstreamed up the Gulf. Messias placed the tiller between upraised calfs, and played with the spreader lines, adjusting the sail to the wind. Although headway across such foul seas was negligible, he was quite satisfied with the sailing capacity of the boat. Bumping along into the late afternoon, he reassessed the situation. If the wind were to blow steady out of the northwest day and night, he reckoned he could make the west coast of Mexico in three days. Along the way he would need water, or enough liquid based nourishment to see him through those days, and longer, if the wind didn't hold. Everything had to fall his way: the wind, the water, the nourishment, but he had no doubt that with this boat he could sail to the coastline of Mexico. I can't expect to be this lucky in the days to come, he thought. The rain was a small gift. I'll need more of the same soon. My food will have to come by way of net, hook, or hand. I might be able to cut a hook from the bony curve of a sailfish gill plate. A fish net of some kind could be woven with the strands of unraveled poly line. There are turtles in these waters, and their blood may be my best source of liquid.

Messias knew that luck played its role, but one never counted on it. Luck ran both ways. He didn't discount luck, but for too long had come to rely on his skills to attach any significance to it. Survival would be a matter of taking advantage of every opportunity and if luck offered up an opportunity or two, all the better.

The wind swirled in directionless gusts as the southerly and northwesterly vied for dominance in the latitude. The declining sun, having settled beneath the curtained hem of the storm, reflected off the water in a pleasing splash of golden warmth. Basking in its final rays, Messias considered the southerly; if it had had a history of sustaining a two or three day blow, I might be inclined to turn around and make for Cerralvo. As it is, this craft could hardly be expected to go to weather. No, my only chance is to sail for the coast. Once the northwesterly returns to strength the going will be better. I'm well south of the Baja peninsula, probably a hundred miles or more southeast of its tip. Somewhere in that open water northwest of Mazatlan.

The sun dipped below the horizon, spraying the storm's puffy trailers in soft ruby reds. The sky and sea sparkled in that cleansing, supernatural glow which follows all storms. Through the diffused light Messias's eyes registered an object that brought him upright on the swim-fined seat; a triangular sail, well south, heading east on a starboard tack. Standing for a better look, he held on to the bill of the sailfish for balance. If I had seen that boat earlier, he thought, I might have been able to close the distance. I have the means to do that now. A standing watch should be taken every hour for boats, working birds, turtles and floating debris.

The sun reflected its last traces in pasteled purples and peach blossom pinks on the cauliflowered residue of the storm. Messias removed the remaining fish strips from their hanging place on the sailfish and impaled them on a single three foot long spine, then lashed the spine to the undersides of the boat's ribs where, in preparation to bake into jerky the following day, they would cure in salt water overnight. Lying back on the swim-finned seat, he watched the first stars glimmer to life in the cloud tarnished blue/black sky.

Twice during the night he was aroused from sleep. Once from a dream of frustration that had him chasing up and down a steep sloped beach trying to pick up scattered dive gear that tide and surf kept sweeping away, and later, when a whale surfaced twenty yards off his bow and exhaled a mighty blow, its flukes flashing their familiar crescent shape in the moonlight before disappearing into the blackened sea. The presence of the moon recalled the previous night with McCorkin, and he laid back down but did not fall directly asleep. The sounds of the night ocean, rising and falling off of itself echoed hollowly, and later, while they softened to familiar music, he fell into dreamless sleep.

❖ 6 ❖

MESSIAS AWOKE WITH THE PALE HINT OF DAY haloing the horizon. He untied the bootie from its place on the aft stay, and sipped two swallows, then abruptly tied it off, fearing that he might drink it all in that moment. An inspection of the hood well for accumulated sea dew was delayed until enough light would insure no accidental spillages. The curing fish strips were pulled, and their shredded cores gave evidence that scavenger fish had fed on them through the night. Reasoning that the putrefying meat had been eaten from around the edges, he selected a large strip, squeezed it of water, and bit off a piece. Although salty, it was fit for consumption and dissolved in mushy clumps. He ate two more strips as the earth spun its way to dawn.

The sun broke white hot on an ocean that had blown itself into fatigued calm. On his knees, he bent to the hooded well where lay a small swallow of sea dew. Tipping the hood he sipped in the liquid and flushed it around, letting it slide down his throat. Licking the sail from arm pit to arm pit, he dispatched the glistening pearls with cat-like thoroughness. The black sail cleansed, he stood and surveyed the surrounding water. The horizon held no boats on his first turn. When he turned again he looked for slight rises across the surface that would indicate turtle or debris. A flock of birds worked a section of water several miles to the northeast—circling, then diving, then taking to the air again—feeding on bait that had been chased to the surface by predator fish. The indication of bait triggered thoughts of a fish net, and Messias wove in his mind the threads of an unraveled length of poly line between two sail-fish spines. Upon further consideration, the idea of an open-ended net, particularly when trying to catch lightning fast bait, didn't make sense. They'd be in and out in a flash. A scoop net would be more practical and the earlier idea of cutting the rim from the gill plate acquired form.

He released the two spreader lines, and tied them to the aft float. Removing his wet suit top, he laid it across the lines for sunshade, and a place to bake into jerky what remained of the fish strips. After laying the cured strips in rows atop the sunshade, he inspected the gill plate for cutting. The delicate tissues of a gill, exposed as they were to external elements, are the first of a fish to turn bad. Those of the sailfish gave off an eye watering stench, and Messias took his breaths through his mouth to escape the smell. The bone-hard cartilage of the gill plate resisted the knife at every stroke, and the boat very nearly capsized in his efforts to free it.

When finally the plate rested in his blue bikinied lap beneath the sunshade, he began to etch out the rim's pattern. Using his third finger as an edge guide, he cut with the point of the knife a three-quarter inch wide rim around the circumference of the eighteen inch diameter plate, working the knife repeatedly over the same line. When a groove had been furrowed, more pressure could be applied without fear of the knife slipping.

By late morning the rim of the scoop was cut away and a three-foot length of poly line had been twisted apart to its strands. Propping himself against the wet suit sail, which pressed into the sailfish, he unraveled a single strand down to its threads until a pile of three-foot long yellow thread lay in his lap. At the rim's mid-point, the first thread was strung and knotted at opposing ends. Working away from the center, he tied each thread a quarter of an inch apart. Rotating the rim so the looping threads ran vertically, he wove in horizontal threads, tying them a quarter of an inch apart.

The sun was well past its zenith, and the fish strips well on their way to jerky when the foot-deep scoop was completed. Anxious to test it and develop an idea how best to wield it underwater, the scavenger fish which had fed on the fish strips and had gathered beneath the boat awaiting further meals, became the prey. Putting on his face mask, Messias slipped over the side. Half a dozen sergeant majors, two to three inches long with black vertical bars imposed on a yellowish/white body, and a tight school of silver jacks, four to five inches in length, jumped at his entry.

Of more value than potential meals, the boat offered the fish a protective cover from the voracious gulls, and they were unwilling to abandon their new found haven at the mere presence of Messias. They hovered defiantly at the boats aft end and not until he moved toward them did they break out into open water. Once clear of the boat, he raised the scoop out of the water and brought it down hard atop the fish. Scattering at the impact, they regrouped at the forward end of the boat. Drifting to them, he tried another rather half-hearted swipe which the fish effortlessly avoided, and which more or less confirmed the futility of the mission. The making of the scoop was but the first small step of this undertaking.

The water was refreshingly cool and in the heat of the windless afternoon, he decided to swim for awhile. Hanging the scoop over the gaping mouth of the sailfish, he removed the swim-finned rudder and seat from their lashings, and tied a line to the aft buoy. Looping the line over a shoulder, he kicked off in an easterly direction with the boat in tow.

A leisurely swim in an open ocean was, even for Messias, an uncommon event. Often he had swum in deep water far removed from land mass, but never without a speargun and the accompanying eye of the hunter.

As the swim progressed, his predator eye gradually loosened its grip on the depths, and transparent strings of pulsating membranes, abundant in the wide open seas, and which earlier had not so much as distracted his fleeting eye, now held his attention. Aglow in prismatic whirlings, they came in shapes of spun cones and woven funnels, and he saw in them the spinnings of magical webs by mythical spiders. A jellied membrane, the length and width of a knuckled joint, stilled his kicks. It caught the rays of sun in its pirouettes, and dazzled with kaleidoscopic colors. A thing of exquisite and delicate beauty, it was unlike anything he had ever seen. From where do such creatures come?, he wondered. And how do they manage to exist in this vast nothingness? The questions fell on the iridescent dancer of light without reply, and Messias resumed his kicking.

The nothingness held his thoughts, and became the bearing on which another unaccustomed turn was taken. It was doubtful there existed another who could be as comfortable as Messias, swimming along in the middle of an open ocean. Although free from the fear that would normally accompany terra firma man in a similar position, there was no denying the vulnerability he felt. The vulnerability, he knew, was rooted in the nothingness, for it represented all that man was not. It existed beyond man, and its presence reduced him to transparent strings of pulsating membranes that occasionally caught the light of the distant sun.

When Messias began to encounter the deep ocean, he was forced to confront this vulnerability and the nothingness from which it was sired. His early introduction to the ocean spared him the plight of many who do not understand that to be vulnerable does not necessarily mean one must also be fearful. This understanding left his eye clear to observe, and his mind free to absorb the surroundings. The nothingness remained, as it must, and his vulnerability became as the water; transparent and accessible to external elements.

Released from the burden of fear, he moved about the environment with a lightness that rendered him equal to the inhabitants, an accomplishment few men could master. And as free as any seal, he came to ask, "Why else would one seek out a wilderness, if not to experience freedom of movement, and to see that movement expressed in the creatures, all flowing in rhythm to the precepts of nature? Precepts, that if one's instincts and intuitions were true, revealed themselves through attentiveness, patience and a willingness to see things as they are."

Messias had traveled many an ocean pathway, and swam up his share of narrow tributaries in search of the ocean's wisdoms, secrets and currents. He understood its laws, and knew no separation from its currents. He attempted to always sense the ocean with the same delicate omniscience with which it sensed him. Thus he moved about its waters with awareness, unencumbered by any notions of alienation.

Alienation, recalled Messias with irony, was all I ever knew as a child.

❖   ❖   ❖

I hated that silver tea set on its silver tray and the smell of the polish and the blackness of the tarnish on my hands.

"Don't stop rubbin'" said Naomi, the Lummi Indian woman that was half nanny and half housekeeper for Doctor Messias and his wife Julie.

"What use are these silver things?" asked Raymond. "No one ever uses them. Most of the stuff here is never used. They have to be cleaned all the time and they're never used."

"I got no way to explain the sense of it," said Naomi. "It's important to your mother. She's no different than the others who live in this part of Bellingham."

"I don't want a mother who cares so much about this junk. I want to be an Indian, like you Naomi."

"You a stange child, Raymond. More Indian than some Indians I know. That's why you're always gettin' into trouble and havin' to polish the silver when you should be outside playin' with the other children."

"Their games are boring. I'd like to be in the woods up on Squallicum Hill, and run as fast as I can on the deer trails, and jump over the dead trees and stumps that hide in the grass."

"You like it in the woods by yourself?"

"I like the sounds that come when I'm by myself. There are things I can hear but can't see. A tree that is full of song, but it's got no birds. The smell of the wind off the sound. I sit for hours and things turn and rustle and come alive. I once saw a stone turn into a squirrel. And a bush become a deer. Everything is slippery and full of surprise. It seems like all the sounds of the woods fly into my chest…But it all goes away when I come home."

"That why you don't come home some nights, eh? Get yourself in all that trouble with your mother and father.

Raymond's heart hurt, and he lowered his head in the shame of the innocent.

"I can't make them understand."

Naomi put down her dust cloth and held out her enormous brown arms and Raymond hurled himself into them, burying his head into her large breasts and loosing himself in the womb of her embrace. "You cryin' out for all the things that's the gift of everyone before they throw them away for somethin' that shines. They trying to take them from you before you even know what there are. Once they're gone, you never get em back. How can a little boy know about such things?"

"What things are you talking about?"

"All the things that tell us who we are. Like that silver tray tells you what your face looks like. The woods are telling you what your heart looks like and what is the face of the Great Spirit."

"What's the face of the Great Spirit look like?"

"I can't tell you that. You got to see it for yourself. Could be a tree, or a fish, or a rock, or your own face. My Great Grandfather says he comes from the Blackfish. When he was your age, seven years old, the Blackfish, what you call the killer whale, took him down to the world under the sea and they took off their Blackfish clothes, and they was men inside. They showed him all the water magic, how to stay under for as long as they liked and how to make boats that moved without paddelin'."

"Do deer and birds wear clothes?"

"Maybe everythin' wears the clothes of somethin' else, eh. All of it is the Great Spirit hidin' from us. Foolin' us all the time. The Lummi Indian used to know this was true but they start thinkin' like the white man an forgot. Now we believe everythin we see. But not you Raymond. You still feelin' everything. Knowin' it without its clothes."

"Did your Grandfather come back?"

"Sure, he come back. He was a human bein' that lived on the land. He didn't have to wear the clothes of an animal. He believed that it was a great privilege to be a human bein' and care for the land, so that all his brothers and sisters of the woods and the waters would always have a home."

"I wouldn't have come back. I would have put on the Blackfish clothes and stayed with them under the water. I don't like being a human. Maybe it'd have been different if I was an Indian way back with your Grandfather.

"Someday soon I take you over to Lummi Island and we watch 'em build the war canoes for the Stommish races."

"What is the Stommish, Naomi?"

"Big ceremony. Used to be long ago, everyone come from far away, all the rich Indians give away their wealth to show how unimportant it was to be rich. They have contests with all the tribes, big war canoes, hold twenty men, would race clear across Puget sound."

"Will you take me soon?"

"Maybe, we'll see, eh. Your mother and father they goin' to have trouble enough with a boy like you. They don't need me to help you along."

"I need you Naomi. Without you, I don't know what I'd do."

Raymond, unable to encircle her waist with his arms, grabbed the rolls of flesh and squeezed.

"You need love, Raymond. Everyone need love. That's what you got me for. Just to hold and love you. Especially when your mother tries to tame you into somethin' you're not supposed to be."

Oblique, silver threaded rays quivered beneath the surface in the late afternoon sun. Weary from the swim, Messias climbed aboard and stretched out the length of the boat. The calves of his legs hung over the aft buoy, and his feet dangled in the water. Before he fell asleep he was feeling the warmth of Naomi's arms.

A breeze freshened out of the northwest, rousing Messias from sleep. Rising for a sea watch, he spotted a dark bulge on the surface two miles north. It might be a seal, he thought, or flotsam, but perhaps it was a turtle. Lowering the sunshade and depositing the fish jerky in the unused water container cut from the calf of McCorkin's wet suit, he swung the boat to a port tack. In the light breeze, the boat barely held a course. Within an hour the developing wind had pushed its speed upwards to two knots. The wind also brought a chop that obscured the object of his search, or it had swum away. In either case, it couldn't be located. Messias guessed that he was less than a half mile from where he last saw it and continued to sail in that direction for another thirty minutes. In that time no further sighting was made, so he came about, resuming his course to Mexico.

Silhouetted against a ringing blue sky, a frigate, black and angular, floated on frozen wings. The water bootie swung from the aft stay. Messias's eyes moved from the frigate to the bootie and back again. The frigate slid south. Messias sailed east, looking at the sky, looking at the sea, looking at the bootie.

Dusk turned the sky a burnt sienna, his thirst the color of the sky. Reaching for the water bootie he reasoned that if he were to wait much longer, dehydration would set in, and what little water there was wouldn't be enough to deter it. Better that he drink it now when it would do some good.

The Mexican sun had done its work on the thin strips of fish meat, baking them into jerky. Taking two, he settled back on the swim-finned seat as strings of pelicans winged their way across a vermillion sky. After chewing the jerky into mash, and drinking the last of the water, he cut two holes in the large container so it could be hung on the aft stay, and loosened its closed end, permitting an air flow to keep the jerky dry for the night.

The breeze of late afternoon had diminished, but refused to die entirely with the daylight. It was not much of a wind, thought

Messias, but not one to ignore either, and he repositioned himself on the ribbed fin, and continued the sail, navigating by way of the northwest swell. Near midnight the wind fell to a zephyr, and in half sleep he tied off the tiller, and laid back against the fish float.

The barren shoreline runs straight as a desert road. The ocean to his right, churning in small, slick, waves, slides smoothly up blinding white sand. The beach inclines gradually to his left then abruptly shears away to white clouded blue. He has been walking for hours. The beach is endless in either direction. The wind-rowed sand gives no trace of his steps, and he wonders if his feet are attached to his legs, and looks to make sure. In the distance the white bones of a beached whale, half buried, rise out of the sand. Its skeleton lays intact and perfect above the high tide mark. The bones twitch to life becoming white gulls that lift from the sand and fly into the sun. A solitary bird convulses at his feet. He reaches for it and the bird becomes ridged in his hand, then turns to porous stone and crumbles away to fine dust.

With whitened hand outstretched he walks into the water and stoops to wash. In knee deep emerald shallows his feet and lower legs are not visible below the water line. The water is thick and viscid. Turning for shore he struggles to move his legs. All energy is required to move an inch at a time. Reaching ankle deep water and thoroughly exhausted, he falls forward to the dry sand, and tries to crawl up the sloping beach. Resting for a moment, he looks down and his feet and lower legs are melting away into the sea, then knees, and thighs dissolve, followed by hips, stomach and chest. In quiet horror, he watches the sea reclaim his body.

Messias awoke and in the moon's yellow light the white beach of his dream appeared. The moon descended into a far sky and he waited for dawn.

❖ 7 ❖

SAVE FOR A HINT OF SWELL that came out of the northwest, dead stillness reigned on both air and sea. The sun broke the horizon like an acetylene torch cracking on. Messias knelt at the altar of the wet suit sail, and bowed his head to the accumulated sea dew. Lapping up a palm-full, he stiffly gained his feet to search out drops that rested on the sail. After licking them away, he perused the fish jerky container, selected a piece and chewed on it while scanning the ocean. The glazed surface was empty of boats, working birds, or floating debris. "Today would be a good day for turtle," he said aloud, "smooth seas and hot."

Lacquered seas and thoughts of turtle evoked a time twenty-five years earlier, when he had first come to the Gulf. The underwater territory was untouched, and overflowed with life. In the company of two other divers they had hired out a panga, which then came with a Mexican guide. The guide had brought along his young son, and together they headed straight out to sea, searching for the slight, almost imperceptible bumps on the surface that indicated turtle.

Three miles offshore, the boy silently raised his arm and pointed south. Everyone strained to catch sight of the turtle. The boat changed course, and was five minutes into its new heading before the others saw the bump on the horizon. It went that way all day. Bets were taken, but no one could spot a turtle before the boy. Messias had never before, or since, witnessed eye sight as keen as the boy's.

They would drift up quietly behind a basking turtle and a diver would jump it from the boat and ride it to exhaustion there in the open ocean. The very large turtles gave wild rides, and sometimes the diver could not control it by lifting its shell behind the head, and guiding it back to the surface. The turtle would dive to depth and the diver would have to let go to resurface for a breath.

Turtle meat was delicious and Messias ate it often, finding it to be the most distinctive and flavorful of all the ocean delicacies.

Over the course of his ocean travels however, he learned that turtles die hard. That their strong hearts kept them alive long into suffering, and that there was probably not another creature on the face of the earth that was treated more cruelly by humans after they had been captured.

Several years after that first turtle hunt, he had been diving off a remote island high in the gulf's mid-riff. Accompanied by two others in an open boat, they were searching out a campsite for the night, and passed a small, isolated beach, a large portion of which was covered by a canvas tarp. The others were not curious as to what secrets lay beneath the tarp and wanted to push on. Messias felt compelled to look. Jumping from the boat, he swam to the beach, and in the heat of a mid-day sun lifted the tarp. Underneath were turtles, alive and on their backs, dried tears caked to their brows, their heads hanging long and awkwardly out of their shells. The suffocating stench of the dead hit him like a punch, and he reeled backwards dropping the canvas.

Returning, he tore the cover from its stake and drug the nearest turtle down to the water, setting it free, then ran up the beach and grabbed another. The two in the boat shouted, demanding that he stop.

"Let it be, this is Mexico. It's a way of life."

He continued dragging the turtles down to the water, releasing them to its coolness. The men in the boat anchored it, and swam ashore. They were wrestling Messias to the ground when three turtle fisherman appeared in their skiff, one angrily flashing a machete, both screaming in Spanish. Forced from the beach, Messias swam back to the anchored boat. They weighed anchor as the fisherman retrieved a turtle still floundering in the shallows. Messias watched them drag it up the beach to the canvas. On that day he renounced the flesh of turtle.

Stripping off the wet suit top, he laid it across the sail trim lines and aft stay, and emptied the container holding the fish jerky on top for another day of drying. A piece nearest the opening and exposed to the night air had become soggy and was thrown overboard. Stretching out on the swim-finned seat he welcomed the morning sun which evaded the shade and struck the length of his body. Basking in its warmth, he explored the material possibilities for the construction of a fish hook.

There was the thin boned gill plate, but there were also the inner workings of the trigger mechanism to consider. The light return spring could easily be molded into a hook, but in these waters the large and powerful fish would easily straighten it. There was the curved trigger, but it, as well as the remaining parts, was of stainless steel and could not be reshaped. The polished stainless buckle that held the strap of McCorkin's face mask was also unworkable, though it might serve well as a lure. There wasn't much. In the old days, the metal frame securing the face plate to the mask might have been worked into something. Today, they are all of plastic. The old wishbones that held the rubber tubing in cocking position on the shaft could have been bent into a perfect hook. Now they are so beefy, nothing less than a hammer and anvil could reshape them. No, there wasn't much.

Removing the gill plate from its place between the fish and the float, he turned it in his hands, examining where it was thinly gauged, and where it graduated to thickness. Cut too thin, and the hook might break during the cutting. Too thick, and it would be bulky for a fish's mouth. A middle range was selected, and a pattern carefully scratched out with the point of the knife, following the same procedure as with the cutting of the scoop.

The work was monotonous and he broke the tedium with frequent standing watches. By mid-morning the fish hook was very nearly cut through, and his only sightings were of birds on the wing. Approaching the final cuts, too much pressure was put to bear near the curve of the hook and it broke. It was almost expected, as he had designed the hook to proportion and during the cutting realized that the stem near the curve was too thin. Better to have designed a wider hook, and then with the edge of the lead weight grind it down to size.

Cutting a fish hook from the gill plate of a sailfish on rolling seas would be difficult. So while smooth seas prevailed, he began again, this time, scratching out a wider stem and curve from a thicker area of the gill plate. As before, the repetitious work was broken with sea watches. Halfway through the cutting, a standing watch disclosed a slight rise in the water to the southwest. Neither the distance to the object, nor the object itself could be determined. He would have to move closer.

After cutting away the remaining gill plate to use for a paddle, he lay on the keel with his chest resting on the aft buoy, and paddled in short, easy strokes. The going was slow, and it took nearly an hour to cover a thousand yards. Standing for a sighting, he identified the shell of a green sea turtle.

Half again as many yards were paddled, which put him within two hundred feet of the turtle. Letting the boat drift, he made final preparations. The fish strips were removed from the sunshade and placed in the large container. The sunshade was reclaimed as a wet suit top for additional buoyancy and protection against the sharp barnacles that generally fasten to a turtle's shell. A pair of gloves, in tatters from the battle with the sailfish, partially covered his hands. Needing a single swim fin to control lift and turns, the one used as a seat was taken. Looping a fifty foot length of poly line across a shoulder and under an arm, he tied the loose end to the wooden stock. After securing the paddles between the fish head and floats, he rested his knees on the aft float, and with back bent at each dip of his hands, silently made his way to the basking turtle.

The boat was within ten feet of the turtle, whose weight he guessed to be near a hundred pounds, when it stirred. Its foreflippers reached out into the water and its head dipped quickly below the surface. At the movement Messias rose and launched himself flat out. One hand caught the upper edge of shell, the other, a piece of rear flipper. In full flight the turtle dove into the sea. Messias worked his left hand to the bottom of the shell, and his right hand to its top behind the head. Pulling back with the right hand, and pushing down with the left, he tilted the shell as an aileron. The turtle resisted, fighting to sustain its descent into the safety of the depths. The laws of aquadynamics prevailed over the turtles determined effort, and a sweeping turn for the surface was executed. Reaching the top, the turtle and the man exhaled simultaneously. The man caught two quick breaths, the turtle one, and they plunged down again. Bending his body at an angle left to right, and at the same time putting pressure left to right with both hands, Messias forced the turtle into a long lopping turn, heading it in an easterly direction. Then shifting his weight, he again pulled back on the shell for another ascent.

The turtle was strong, as turtles are, and its flippers surged powerfully through the water in quick, arching sweeps. Messias was able to level out its flight at a depth of fifteen feet, which seemed to suit the turtle, and at half-minute intervals, he pulled back on the shell forcing it to the surface for a breath. The turtle grew accustomed to this pattern and, finding a rhythm of breathing that matched Messias's needs, began to respond to lighter hand pressure on its shell.

It was in this manner that the sea creature and its rider traveled toward the western coast of Mexico.

Messias was at his best with the turtle, moving under the water at swim speed, surfacing for the intermittent breath. He would have been content to travel a hundred miles in this fashion.

Sensing that the turtle knew its fate, Messias was in no rush to end its last flight. In the limpid sky of the cloudless open ocean they flew as one. Messias spoke to the turtle, telling it that he knew it was presenting itself as a gift, and that he was grateful and would not kill such a spirited creature were it not for his own survival. He could not know if the turtle understood, but if its movement were an indication then it seemed so.

The turtle carried the man and towed the boat for well over an hour. Its strong heart reflected in its stamina and willful endurance. Gradually it succumbed, and when all physical resources had been depleted, it stopped swimming and lay on the surface breathing in whizzing gasps, its flippers hanging listlessly at its sides. Messias slipped the line from his shoulder, and tied it to the turtle's left hind flipper. Returning to the boat he relashed the swim fin to the keel, and reattached the wet suit top to the aft stay for a shade, and made ready the two water tight containers.

Pulling the turtle gently to the boat, he again spoke to it, openly thanking it for its life. Then lifting it half out of the water, and tilting it against a bent leg, he drew his knife, and cut hard across the reptilian skin at the throat. Dark blood spurted from the incision. The turtle thrashed weakly as Messias placed a bootie beneath the severed artery. When the foot of the bootie filled, he lifted it to his mouth and drank. The blood had a thick, chalky, consistency, not as salty as he expected. Crimson streaks skated down his chin and he repositioned the bootie under the still-spurting neck. A second bootie was filled, drunk and chased by a hand scoop of ocean water while a darkened pool of blood spread about the boat.

The sharks will be here soon, thought Messias, dragging the turtle up onto the ribs of the boat where he caught another bootie of blood, which was hung on the aft stay. The flow of blood had ebbed to a steady ooze, and he tied the turtle, shell side down, to the wooden stock and paddled away from the spoor.

Messias paddled east, as always. After awhile he stood to guage his progress, marking his point of departure where careening shark fins cut the newly discovered blood spoor. It wouldn't take much for them to sniff me out, he reasoned, noting the blood still dripping from the turtle's neck. They would come right out of the water for this turtle. An hour of paddling was put between the shark and the see-through craft before he stopped to measure the turtle for butchering.

Butchering a turtle is a messy, difficult business. He had seen it done enough times, but never experienced it first hand. There was that tough reptilian skin, and all that bone and gristle to cut and chisel through. Beginning cautiously, he sawed off the flippers close to the shell, dulling the knife in the process, and turning the work strenuous when it came to cutting through the leather-like bindings that held the belly plate to the shell. He sawed and hacked until the bindings severed, freeing the belly plate, and exposing the attached calipee. Scooping out the gelatinous yellow substance, he ate until filled. Then he gouged three holes in the slick belly plate and lashed it to the keel, replacing the swim-finned seat. Sitting in relative comfort, he cut deep into the turtle. Gristle and tendon flew from his knife, and eventually the scraps drew three sharks and a score of sea gulls. The circling sharks snatched up the few bits that escaped the sharp-eyed gulls.

Messias ate pieces of raw turtle as he worked. The stringy, red meat had a delicate sea food taste and offered more substance than fish. After drinking the blood and eating the calipee, his shrunken stomach had little room for the meat so the bulk of it was laid atop the sunshade where it would bake into jerky. The nutritious calipee and thirst quenching blood brought new energy, and he worked steadily into late afternoon. The turtle's four shoulders produced pockets of meat, and the stomach was removed and cleaned to serve as a bootie lining, insuring a leak-proof container. He scrapped the shell of its cartilage, and pried out what he could of the spinal column, sucking its marrow.

The shark count had risen to six, including two large hammerheads. There was no trace of blood in the water, and the sharks didn't appear twitchy, though they moved with purpose. They'll likely stay with the boat through the night, thought Messias. He had plans for restructuring the boat using the turtle shell as a bow and affixing the floats to either side of it, giving the boat a broader beam to improve stability and sailing efficiency. The sharks prevented that from occurring, so he gouged four holes in the shell, one at each corner, to later secure the floats, and lashed it to the port ribs, amidships, where it would serve as an outrigger for the night.

After finishing this last task near dusk Messias reclined back on the smooth surface of the belly plate, which was considerably more comfortable than the ribbed swimfin, and watched the sharks and gulls circle the boat in that tireless pace given to scavengers, their triangled fins and wings cutting evenly through the smooth water and air in patient anticipation of a final meal. A curious shark nosed the lashed turtle shell, and he jabbed it away with a length of fish spine.

Dusk struck the sky a bright claret, and when the last gull broke east for land fall, Messias stood for a final watch. Three miles to the south a trawler shuffled its way west. It was the same white and green sharker he and McCorkin had seen; two, three days ago? The sighting revived that odd feeling of foreboding felt earlier. Despite the calm seas he knew his low silhouette couldn't be seen at this distance, and he made no effort to attract the boat. It tracked across the blazing sunset, engulfing itself in the reflected flames of the extinguished sun.

Unsure of how long the turtle blood would remain drinkable, he untied the bootie and tipped it. The blood had coagulated and poured from the bootie in fleshy clumps. Rinsing it out, he transferred the last pieces of fish jerky to it, and placed the turtle meat in the large open-ended container, stringing them both to the aft stay. The incoming tide of darkness consumed the last vestiges of the sunset and he put on the wet suit top and stretched the length of the boat, falling asleep before Orion had strung his lighted belt.

❖ 8 ❖

MESSIAS AWOKE FROM A SOUND SLEEP to the sound of music. Lying with eyes wide, and a near-full moon filling them, the music wafted across the tranquil sea. "Am I dreaming this music?," he asked aloud. Rising to a sitting position and facing in the direction of the music, he saw, not a mile away, lit up like an all-night supermarket, a large ship moving easterly at a fast clip. Immediately he recognized it to be the Baja to mainland ferry, traveling from La Paz to Mazatlan. He had been on that ferry, or one like it, and had tried to sleep in his car during the crossing and a radio had played all night. The bridge of the vessel was clearly visible, as were figures moving under the lights. Even if they were looking for me, which they're not, he thought, I'm too low in the water for their radar. These days there are no top-side watches. They stay warm in the navigation room and search for blips on the radar screen. If no blips appear, then an object doesn't exist. McCorkin is probably right. I won't be found until someone runs over me and I jam up their prop. Laying back down, he listened to the music until it faded into sea sounds.

Messias couldn't sleep. The irony of the musical ferry did not escape him; the ferry and those on board heading in the same general direction, while he in his make-shift craft, headed down a path distinctly his own. However dangerous that path might be, in truth, he would have it no other way; it could be no other way.

The blows came in stinging shocks to his back and neck. "Take his pants." And hands stopped their punches and grappled for the buckle of his belt. Raymond dropped his hands from his face and reached for his pants. The giggles of girls further encouraged the boys that now had pulled his pants to his knees and were tearing away his underwear. Raymond doubled up as all stood away and laughed mockingly. A voice from outside the circle shouted, "Break it up, what the hell's going on here?" Raymond yanked up his pants and only then did tears fill his eyes.

The children ran off in all directions as Emmet Singleton bent down to Raymond.

"You all right, Raymond?"

"Yeah, I guess so."

"This is the third time this month, Raymond. We got to put a stop to this. Them high school boys got nothin' better to do.

I'm goin' to call their parents and tell 'em to leave you alone or I'm callin' the cops"

"I don't know why they do it..."

"They're bullies Raymond. Cowards, really. Shouldn't be pickin' on somebody still in Junior High."

"They wait for me."

"They're afraid of you, Raymond."

Raymond laughed and shook his head in disbelief.

"You're different from 'em. You look 'em in the eye an tell 'em to fuck off. They can't scare you."

"But they do scare me. I don't like walking by this block, I'm always afraid they'll start in on me."

"Yeah, maybe so Raymond, but you still walk by here. You could go around over to State street, but you walk this way every day, even though you're scared. Down deep that scares the shit out of 'em. Can you get home all right?"

"Thanks, Emmet."

"Sure...Sorry about Naomi."

Raymond looked up at Emmet as though a great pain had struck him in the stomach.

"What happened to Naomi?"

"I heard your mother kicked her out today. Big trouble. She went back to the reservation."

Emmet paused, "You didn't know?" Raymond was up and sprinting towards home.

"Where's Naomi?" asked Raymond, trying to keep his voice from shaking.

The arctic blue eyes of his mother glared at him. "She got very sick, and she won't be coming back."

For reasons he could never understand, Raymond always sensed deceit in others, and in his mother it brought particular pain.

"Just once, why don't you tell me the truth," shouted Raymond,

His mother turned so quickly that she frightened him, as was her intention. Through a smiling, twisted, mouth she spat her words.

"Don't be cheeky with me. Naomi was here too long and was a very bad influence in this home. Things are going to be different from now on. There shall be no more excursions to Lummi Island. No more days of skipping school and running off to the hills or wherever it is you go. No more notes of excuse from Naomi. You have become an embarrassment to both your father and me and we intend to put an end to it."

And so they did. Everything changed after Naomi left. It was as if the sun had gone down and never reappeared again.

Raymond endured the separation from Naomi for nearly a year before he packed a bag and rode the bus to the Lummi Reservation.

On a broken down, unpainted, porch she took him in her arms and held him for a long time while a black and white dog sniffed his shoes. "Come inside child, I'll fix you coffee."

The single room was large. The walls were plastered with curled pictures of Indian faces torn from the pages of magazines. In the middle of the room was a table with an ironing board and a wash tub on it. In one corner stood an old refrigerator that was dark with grime. On its top were stacked crudely woven baskets with wooden figures peeking out of dark openings. A stove that was once yellow rested in the other corner of the room; its oven door lay broken and resting on a single hinge. A lone, pillowless, sheetless, matteress lay near the stove. Flies circled madly above the table that Naomi cleared. She collected two chairs that had scattered to opposite ends of the room.

"I can't stay in Bellingham anymore," said Raymond. "The kids at school talk like their parents. They believe everyone thinks the same way they do. They listen to the teachers instead of the tide. Whatever the teacher says, even if it's wrong, is right."

Raymond paused to sip from a chipped ceramic cup. He sighed heavily, realizing that the burdens he had been carrying for so long could not so easily be discarded. His voice registered a weariness that did not go unnoticed by Naomi.

"Lately I'm beginning to wonder," he continued, "if I'm going crazy. Am I the only one that hears the tide and sees the wind?"

Raymond paused for a moment and sipped his coffee. "That's why I came to see you."

Naomi studied Raymond while gulping coffee from a big metal cup, then put down the cup and touched his tousled hair and looked into his intense dark eyes. He would soon become a man, she thought. She knew that what she was about to say would change his life, and not necessarily for the better.

"You got a hard road in front of you, Raymond. Harder'n most, that's for sure. But you got the chance of living beautiful too. You need a place to go where you can be at peace. Somewhere in the wilderness where you can live by the truths you have figured out. You've found out that when you get old, everyone loses the truths they learned as a kid. They start to believe that books know more'n the woods or the water. Trouble is, nobody knows nothin' about the woods or the water anymore. So they don't have no truths to lose. The white man needs somethin' he can hold in his hands, or in his brain. He don't know things can be known in the heart and in the stomach and listened to with the eyes."

The Indian woman put her hands on either side of the boy's face and looked directly into his eyes. He reached up and held her warm brown arms.

"The sounds I carry in my heart and behind my eyes have become small," he said. "I'm afraid they'll go away."

"Them sounds are your truths. They belong to you and you got to listen to 'em. The white man's world is complicated. He make it that way so he can push the gentle ones off to one side and confuse 'em so they don't make trouble with the real truth. The real truth scares 'em because its got to do with the things they can't see or understand. That's why they made an enemy out of nature."

"What am I going to do?"

"You got to go back. I can't keep you here. This place gets old mighty fast. You go back and every night you remember something that the woods and the water taught you. You keep it inside of you, no matter what anyone says or does. But don't tell 'em what you doin' or what you think. You do this and you wait. One day you find a way back into the wilderness and then you go quick and don't come back. You do that, you be all right."

The following year the family left Bellingham for the Gold Coastline of Southern California, and Raymond never saw Naomi again nor did he return to the woods of Squallium Hill, or the waters of Puget Sound. When he discovered the kelp forests in the warm waters of the Pacific Ocean two blocks from his home in Corona del Mar, he knew it was the place Naomi had predicted he would find. He escaped into the ocean world and resurrected his spirit. The secrets of the birds and deer became the secrets of the fish and seals. The abundant ocean filled him with its pure wilderness. For the second time in his young life he was set free to seek out the face of the Great Spirit.

"I've seen the face of the Great Spirit and now there's nothing left for me," Messias said aloud. "Is this where I am to die? If it's time for me to die, why am I trying so hard to live?" Messias had always believed that he would die as quickly and as cleanly as the ocean deaths he had witnessed. Dying of thirst or starvation was not the swift death he envisioned. It permitted too much time to think, as he was doing now. It was easier to die doing something than to die doing nothing. "So do I hang on and die of thirst," he said aloud, "or do I throw myself to the sharks? Do I fight to live? Do I want to live? Yes, but I'm not sure why."

Fully awake, he studied the stars, taking mental notes of the ferry's direction in relationship to them. If ever the wind were to rise during the night, he could point the boat to that star chain below the belt of Orion, and it would lead him to Mazatlan.

❖ 9 ❖

DAWN EMERGED FROM DARK TO LIGHT in a steady progression of primary blues. Messias knelt on the belly plate before a hyacinth sky, and tilted the hood to his lips. Downing a swallow, he wobbled to his feet to lick the sail. Completing his rounds, he lifted a strip of fish jerky from the bootie and gnawed on it as the sun broke the horizon at cone ten. Reflecting off a slick sea, its brilliance painfully constricted the pupils of his bloodshot eyes. Shutting them to the pain, he inched back down to the belly plate as a thousand blue suns cavorted about the insides of his eyelids. The boat drifted in slow circles, and he chewed on the last strip of dried fish. Feeling the sun's warmth on his back, he reopened his eyes. To the windless calm he said, "Another good day for turtle," and stood again. The horizons claimed no boats, nor working birds, nor any sign of curious lumps in the water. The gleaming sea, absent of the sharks of yesterday evening, encouraged the installation of the turtle shell bow. The project would be a major operation. Everything must come down—the sail, the stays, the sailfish head—everything.

Releasing all stays, the sailfish head was lowered onto the aft buoy and secured. The wet suit was laid across the sailfish, and the drying turtle meat placed to the sun. The forward floats, free of the sailfish, were separated and released to either side of the inverted turtle shell by way of holes gouged out the day before. The combined floatation raised the reattached speargun stock another three inches above the water line, providing nearly six inches of freeboard at its highest point. The sailfish head, which had begun to deteriorate, was placed in the well of the shell and relashed in its upright position. All stays were refastened and adjusted, and by late morning the boat was balanced and ready to sail. The only element missing was wind.

While calm seas prevailed, Messias resumed work on the second fishhook. He followed the already scratched out pattern for a wider, thicker, hook. Through the morning he worked and as the sun reached its apex the hook was cut away from the plate. Using the pitted edge of a lead weight, he ground the hook to an eight inch width, and gave it a razor-sharp point. At the top of the hook's stem a knob was left to affix the poly line thread. He began to twist down a hundred foot length of poly line to its threads. By late afternoon a mountainous pile of yellow thread laid atop the belly plate. Lifting a loose end from the tangled nest he snapped it apart gauging its tensile strength to be about fifteen pounds. It might hold a bullet tuna, he thought, but I'd have better luck with a small dorado. He fastened one end of the thread to the knob of the hook, and above the knob, the stainless buckle from McCorkin's face mask was tied as a lure. Coiling the line, he placed it along with the hook and its lure in the well of the turtle shell for future use.

Cat's paws skipped across the water indicating a mild breeze out of the northwest. Within an hour the breeze had generated enough velocity for a sail and Messias assumed his position in the center of the boat, trimming the sail to the northwesterly.

The sailing efficiency of the craft had improved tenfold. The turtle shell bow fairly skimmed across the water and Messias, for really the first time, felt the sensation of movement. It lifted him into song and he cut across the water singing snatches of a Bob Marley tune to which he knew neither the beginning nor the end. "Three little birds flew by my window, singin' sweet songs, singin', this is my message to you who who. Don't worry 'bout a thing, cause every little thing, gonna be all right."

The wind held into dusk. A China-red sun submerged into a crimson sea and as the last spark of direct sunlight was about to be snuffed out, a pod of orcas surfaced off the port beam. Their dorsal fins, like black sails, cut before the tiny boat. There were four in the pod and they kept to their course, ignoring the flimsy craft that bobbed fifty feet away.

"Blackfish," shouted Messias, "take off your clothes."

There was not another creature on the face of the earth that so impressed Messias than the orca. For sheer power, size, intelligence, and resourcefulness displayed in the stalking of prey, it had no match.

Messias had first seen the orca demonstrate its masterful hunting skills when crossing the Indian Ocean off of Southern Australia. He and a crew of divers were drawn to a flock of working birds, and moved closer to inspect explosions of white water erupting beneath the circling birds. Approaching to within several hundred yards they saw the white water to be the result of orcas leaping high out of the water and returning with a thunderous crash. Sounds of animal bellowing, like screams, resounded across the water. The pod had circled a herd of sea lions preventing their escape. Through the middle of the congested, fear-filled herd, a single orca erupted carrying a bellowing sea lion in its jaws. The sea lion shrieked its terror, blood spurting in all directions, staining the white of the orca's lower jaw.

The massacre was as intelligent as it was brutal. The ease and dispatch with which these "killer whales" fed on the sea lions was testament that the orcas, if they so chose, could attack the boat and devour its occupants with equal facility. Those on board grew apprehensive, and Messias, oblivious to their concern, watched in fascination. It was decided that the boat be moved to a safer distance and Messias protested, knowing that the orcas wouldn't attack, but was given no say over their rule, and the spectacle, for viewing purposes, came to a close.

A decade later Messias made his only underwater contact with an orca while diving alone off Carmen Island, near Loreto in the Gulf. The buoy end of his trailing line had hung up and unable to see its end, he tried to yank it free. With sudden force it was pulled in the opposite direction. Swimming back to investigate, he very nearly ran head-long into a full-grown orca that was holding the buoy in its smiling mouth. The orca tossed the buoy into the air, and nosed it around the water. Messias had the line in his hand and gave it a jerk, pulling the buoy toward him. The orca, accepting the invitation, followed and picked it up and swam off.

Messias tugged hard on the line again, pulling the buoy from its mouth. The orca turned, chased it down and picked it up. They played the game for several minutes before the orca, as if called, swam off in a rush.

Like mammals of the land, the orcas were in possession of qualities that elevated them above those in their family. Among fish the white sea bass was such a creature, an ultra-sensitive pelagic that moved like a free swimming ghost along the California kelp beds in the spring and summer. In the early days of blue water hunting, before the hunters had ventured into the far water for tuna, and wahoo, and other deep ocean fish, the white sea bass, because of its extreme sensitivity to intruders, was the most difficult fish to stalk, and thus became the fish that pushed the limits of a hunter's skill. Messias hunted no other fish. Over a fifteen year period, the white sea bass taught him everything it knew.

Hunting, by its nature, is an aggressive act. Yet, it was this very aggressiveness which the white sea bass so acutely sensed. Messias discovered that aggression, be it in thought or in action, met with immediate departure of the fish. Further, he found that approaching the fish successfully often came down to his mental disposition at the moment of a sighting. Thus he disciplined himself to move about the water without aggression and sustained a mentality that didn't so much attack the ocean as simply observe it with detachment.

It was in this state that he began to receive what he called "impulses." In the haze of the California waters he would "hear" a swimming fish beneath him, beyond visibility, and diving blindly into the murk, would discover a white sea bass. "Dive in this section of water," whispered the voice of the sea, and reaching a particular depth, a fish would pass. Coming to trust the voice even when it went against all logic, he brought in fish where there was said to be none. He observed fish in areas where others saw nothing. His reputation grew and his techniques were studied. He openly spoke of the emptiness of mind and the ocean voice that directed him. The other hunters tolerated his view, but none believed it. They agreed that Messias was a keen observer and a deep diver, but this business of sensing or intuiting the fish was a product of his renowned eccentricities.

It wasn't until the last half-dozen years that these same skeptical hunters began to venture into the deep reaches of the ocean where they encountered tuna, wahoo, dorado, sailfish, and marlin. These open-water fish were more sensitive to intrusion than were the white sea bass, and virtually impossible to get close to. After a period of set-back and failure, they reported that the instant an aggressive thought registered in their minds, the fish would break off its course and swim out of range. It was a phenomenon that conjured a great deal of speculation. Some felt that it was the highly developed lateral line which these open water fish possessed, picking up every vibration the hunter emitted. Others believed that the body language of the hunter betrayed him. Still others believed that a form of telepathy was at play. There was never complete agreement. All did agree that something was occurring beyond anything they could fully understand. As their experience eventually bore out, the only way around it was to do as Messias had long ago suggested — clear the mind and maintain detachment from the unfolding event.

Only a free-diving spearfisherman would know these things, thought Messias, watching the orcas swim after the fallen sun. The scuba diver would have no knowledge of them. He was never exposed to such fish, and his noisy technology was more a liability than a asset.

The pod of orcas disappeared where the magenta sky met with the plum-colored sea. Standing on the belly plate, Messias worked on a piece of dried turtle meat, chewing it into stringy shreds.

"I'll need another turtle soon" he said to the vacant skies. "Two turtles would give me a cushion. I could go four, maybe five days with two turtles; turtles, or rain or lots of fish and wind, always wind."

Storing the jerkied turtle in the open-ended container for the night, he then tied off the tiller and secured the spreader lines, and in the fading light put on the wet suit top.

Darkness rose from the sea like a phantom, spiking the sky with points of light above the lost horizon.

The restaurant is empty and, save for the shuffling steps of many feet, quiet as a tomb. He sits alone at a table set in sterling, fine crystal, and Wedgewood tableware. The waitresses move as if on roller skates, some carry trays of dishes filled with steaming food, others with trays of empty dishes. The smell of food causes him to drool, and saliva runs uncontrollably down his chin. A waitress bends to his face and asks what he will have for dinner. Before he can respond, she says he will need a menu and leaves. He waits but she doesn't return. Hailing another waitress, he asks for a glass of water. She brings to the table a stainless pitcher that drips with condensation, and pours a liquid that is the color of blood. She overfills the glass and it spills down onto the white linen tablecloth. Ignoring the spillage, he raises the glass and drinks. For a moment there is the sensation of refreshment, but the liquid is hot and has scalded his mouth. Leaping from the chair he searches the restaurant for water. Finding none, he rushes for the door and bursts outside where blistering heat sucks the breath from his lungs. Sand dune upon sand dune roll to the horizon. Running to the highest dune, he searches for some sign of greenery, some indication of water, but the colorless desert falls infinitely on. Turning, he retreats to the restaurant, but it has vanished. Tears well and slide down his cheeks. He tries to catch them in his hand and lift them to burnt lips, but they slide away like balls of mercury, and fall into the sand, turning to steam.

❖ 10 ❖

MESSIAS LICKED HIS LIPS and attempted to clear the dream from his throat, but his thirst held it there, and dry swallows tattooed it into permanence. Unmoving, he laid on the belly plate parched from the inside out. The moon's reflection danced in rhythm on the smooth, elongated swells, hypnotically pulling him into its waltzing light. He dozed off and when he awoke, his thirst was as the dream had left it. In prolonged darkness, he waited for morning light, and the sea's dewed offering.

In the horizon's glow, he knelt to the single swallow that laid at the bottom of the hood well. It went down as dust, and the licking of the droplets became a kind of torment. After his tongue completed its rounds across the neoprene, he leaned against the sailfish, whose putrefying smell no longer offended, and looked out across the featureless sea.

Unruffled by wind, the surface shined like glazed lapis. Scouring the cloudless horizons in three-sixty turns, no boats, nor birds, nor lumps of unknown things halted his flying eye. Removing the wet suit top, he laid it across the aft stay and spreader lines, and selected a piece of dried turtle meat and gnawed on it while a flock of pelicans, in their customary V formation, winged their way south. As they faded to an indistinguishable line on the horizon he reclined on the belly plate where the low sun warmed his full length. "It will be hotter today than yesterday," he said, feeling the sun's heat. "If there's no wind, I should slip into the water between ten and two to keep cool."

Messias rocked in the gentle rise and fall of the ocean, drifting in and out of sleep. Awakening, he would stand and scout the surface, then lay down again. In the early afternoon a flock of gulls worked the water a mile to the southeast. The dead air required that he paddle to the diving birds and after ten minutes of paddling in the direct sun, its heat drove him into the water. The ocean was cool and the swim welcomed. Swimming at an easy pace, he marked bearings on the birds during the swim. Closing to several hundred yards a last look disclosed near-empty sky. The birds had settled on the water. Apparently, the predator fish that had driven the bait to the surface had moved on, leaving them to their migrations in the depths. Having come this far, Messias reasoned that it was at least worth an inspection so swam on. Near the edge of the floating birds scattered bait flashed below. There was no sign of a central school, nor any sign of predator fish. The darting bait was on its way out. The gulls eyed him and paddled off to safe distances, knowing to the inch how far the intruder could come before flight was considered. Messias breast stroked to within thirty feet of the resting gulls. Their close proximity raised questions of food and of what use could be put to beak, bones and feathers?

Placing himself between the boat and the birds, he released the tow line, inhaled deeply, and behind the cover of the turtle shell, sank beneath the water. Dropping to a depth of twenty feet he leveled off and swam toward the center of the flock. Well inside its circumference, he slowly rose. Dozens of pink, webbed, feet protruded through the ceiling. Picking out a pair directly overhead, he ascended with arms outstretched intending to grab the feet, drag the bird under, and wring its neck before the sharp bill could wreck havoc on his face and head. (Messias held high regard for a sea gull's rapier beak, having once seen three gulls dive on a jack rabbit which had wandered too near a nest, and kill it in a matter of seconds.) The extended hand was inches from the hanging feet, fingers stretched to grab, when the feet splashed once and disappeared. Breaking the surface, Messias sent the entire flock to the air screeching and hawking in displeasure. In shrugging acceptance he floated back to the boat and climbed under the sunshade as the gulls circled non-stop in protest. During the long swim, he had swallowed salt water that invariably leaks around the mouth piece of a snorkel, and the back of his tongue probed a raw and swollen throat. Having drunk but a cup and a half of water and two pints of turtle blood in twenty-four hours, the combined heat and salt water ushered in the first stages of dehydration. Closing his eyes from the despair of the present, he wandered to the comfort of his past.

"I'm not asking you to give up your ocean", she said. He scarcely heard her words. The softness of her skin consumed him. The smell of her body made him drunk.

"You could move in with me and just try it for awhile," she continued. "See if you like it."

He did not answer. His brown, scarred, hands were feeling the silkiness of her hair, and he was thoroughly distracted at the texture of it running through his fingers.

"It will be a nice change from your boat; a warm bed, home cooked meals, your own shower, closet space. There are advantages. You might even come to enjoy it."

He knew the lightness of his body under the water, but the lightness he was feeling here in this bed was of another kind. He drifted as if in dream. He had been alone far too long, and it was only in this moment that he realized the depths of his isolation.

"I don't know how such a wonderful man could have stayed so single for so long. You are the dream of every woman, Ray Messias. I want you to teach me everything you know about the sea. And I will show you my world. There is so much out there for us; food, music, theater, friends. Brilliant friends, artists, writers, my art gallery draws the best of them. They are fascinating people. All very influential. You could do very well by them. I'll guide you over the bumps. You can have it all."

He heard the music of her voice and it came as a soft and lilting melody from her full mouth. Her lips formed words that were like flowers springing from the earth, fluttering in warm swirling gusts. He needed her love. He needed her love more than ever now; more than hope, or money, or wisdom, or the sea. He needed to drown in her love and sink beneath the surface of an unbearable world. They didn't need air. They would breathe the other's sweet breath and never need the harsh wind of the world again.

In that first year he did not miss the sea. He would look at it and tell her what lay beneath, and she would marvel at his knowledge. She adored his ability to live off the sea. They ate delicious meals of scallop, lobster, abalone, and fish. "You move like a sea lion in the water. You're an incredible sight to see," she once said.

In the second year, his shoes pinched his feet and the tie and tight collar squeezed his voice. He entered the office and sunk into the pearl gray carpet. The floor to ceiling windows behind the desk cast a glare from the smog-filled air of Los Angeles that was nearly blinding. The man behind the desk rose and extended his hand and she introduced them.

"Max, you remember Ray Messias, from Serge's opening last month."

"Yes, of course. Serge always does such wonderful things with negative space. Don't you agree, Ray?"

Messias nodded his head, and glanced at a Picasso hanging alone on the gray wall in the midst of his cubism, and for a moment tried to make some sense of it.

Max swept his arm around to the window and the ghostly shapes of L.A.'s high rises. "This is were it's all happening, Ray. Right here, the center of the world, the core of art, money and beautiful people. Everyone comes here to get rich, because this, as Willie Sutton once said when asked why he robs banks, 'is where they keep the money.' L. A. is the place, and no doubt you want a piece of it."

Messias cast another look at the Picasso.

"Of course he wants a piece of it, Max. That's why we're here. Thought we'd come directly to the vault."

"Yes, the vault," said Max, "quite good. The vault indeed. Well Ray, I've been informed by your most ardent admirer here, that you've been out of the mainstream for awhile and are looking to jump back in."

Messias nodded and Max continued. "I believe in getting away for awhile. I admire those who can do it. You have a background in sales? In L.A. you've got to be able to sell a seat in church to a whore."

"Ray had his own business," she said quickly, "in charter boats. As you well know Max, running your own business is selling all the time."

"Indeed. We have a territory that has recently opened up. Radio stations will be your primary targets. They do a great deal of advertising. Give you a chance to mix with the local D. J.'s. A wild bunch here in L. A. You'll have an ample expense account. These people expect to be entertained."

She went over to Max and placed her arms around him, and kissed him on the cheek. "You're a dear, Max."

"You've got a great lady here, Ray. There's a rumor that you're going to make the leap into martial bliss soon."

She turned from Max and embraced Messias, looking directly into his face. "It's still a rumor. But we might change that at any moment."

Messias glanced at the Picasso to see if there was anything at all in the picture he could recognize.

Rippled prints of a late afternoon breeze galloped across the surface. The sea had come to life and its chop aroused Messias. Lowering the sunshade, he trimmed the sail and tied off the spreader lines.

The developing wind barely pushed him along, but within an hour the turtle shell was cutting across the surface in fine form. The sensation of movement had an uplifting effect, and Messias laid out thirty feet of yellow fishing line, slip knotting it to the port stay.

The wind held into the sunset, then abruptly died. He tied off the tiller and lifted a strip of turtle jerky from its container, and sprawled across the belly plate gazing into a primrose sky. Thinking that food might relieve his aching head, he bit off a piece of turtle, but without saliva to break down the stringy meat, it balled up into a nest of brown threads and twigs, and he spit the mess into the sea.

An evening chill came and in near darkness he put on the wet suit top and waited for sleep. Although exhausted, sleep wouldn't

come and he laid in the neither world between sleep and wake-
fulness for hours. A noticeable thump against the side of the boat
snapped him to alertness. A shark, three times the length of the
boat laid alongside the open ribbed craft, its dorsal fin rising two
and a half feet out of the water, the tip well above Messias's head.
He observed it with indifference, figuring that if the thing had
had a notion to tear into the turtle shell it would have happened
by now. Large sharks settling alongside boats in the open ocean
was nothing new. Some stayed with a vessel for days, even weeks,
feeding on garbage and debris tossed overboard.

The ocean washed over the shark's broad back, and the moon,
rising from the inky water, cast its light evenly across its slick skin.
The moon, magnified by the earth's atmosphere, was as wide as the
shark was long. Messias watched the moon rise and shrink. It was
nearly full now and its glow brought a surreal twilight that would
have sent many a nocturnal creature scurrying back to its lair. Also
seeking the refuge of darkness, Messias closed his eyes again.

❖ 11 ❖

THE MOON HAD DEPARTED and taken the shark with it. There
was a hint of light in the east and when its luminescence permitted, he sucked the dampness from the hood of the wet suit. The
swallow slid empty down his throat. He would need fluid today,
or the dehydration that had him in its grip would soon render
him into incapacitation.

The southern skies, blue and cloudless, showed no indication
of a storm. The sea was as empty of life as the sky of clouds. Only
the wind pulsated with possibilities.

Near mid-morning the earlier portent of wind materialized,
and Messias trimmed the sail to the northwesterly. Just past noon
he changed course to south by southeast at the sight of diving

birds. Running with the wind, the boat made excellent headway and covered a two mile distance in less than an hour. Scores of sea gulls were actively feeding when he arrived, as many more sat atop the surface tranquilly digesting their morning meal. Boils of bait sporadically broke the water in crystal eruptions, the overhead sun reflecting brightly off their silver bodies as they arched in brief flight. Putting on the face mask, he dipped over the aft buoy. Broken schools raced helter-skelter below. Paddling the boat among the birds, which scattered to respectful distances, he searched the water for the heart of the school covering an area the size of a baseball diamond. Small pockets of bait repeatedly broke the surface, but no central body of the school could be located.

Lifting the fish scoop from the mouth of the sailfish, he slipped into the water. Holding the boat with his off hand, the scoop was at the ready in the other. To try and chase the bait down would be fruitless. The only sensible approach was to wait on the surface until the bait swam closely by and take a swipe at them.

Long and sleek, like an oversized barracuda, a wahoo glided by in the limpid water. Its lightening speed and treacherous set of teeth were the stuff of fisherman's tales, and when Messias first saw it, the spearless hunter uttered a sigh of frustration through his snorkel tube. The hook and line would do nothing with this fish. If its teeth didn't sever the line, then it would take all there was and break it off at the end.

The wahoo fed in a deceptive, almost nonchalant way. Lingering about the water, they either hung motionless, or moved slowly, lulling the bait into a state of complacency. Suddenly striking like a thunderbolt, they would burst the school into a shower of silver shrapnel, then casually return to snatch up those which fluttered helplessly in their wounds. If the bait had any chance at all, it was in their numbers and a fleeting disappearance on the other side of the ceiling.

A smattering of bait moved under the boat, seeking refuge from the wahoo and the diving gulls. Messias swung the scoop out and brought it down hard over the top, scattering the bait in all directions. Rather than run for open water, they regrouped at the far end of the craft, more willing it seemed to take their chances with Messias and his scoop than with the gulls and wahoo. Resisting another swipe, he thought it better to offer this refuge in friendship so that more might seek it out; thus he waited, and watched the bait run below in quicksilver rivers.

A tight school swam closely by, an unseen wahoo giving chase. The scoop was dropped, and in mid-flight the bait neatly altered course flicking past the opened net.

The boat continued to draw more fish into its protective custody. Messias waited and watched. Fish raced every which way, several times breaking surface yards away.

A dense ball of bait, which appeared as a single, silver-scaled entity, charged up from below. The first to reach the surface avoided the net, but the mass behind, blind to what was in front of them and pushed by those closest to the wahoo, plowed forward. They bounced off his body, crashed into his face mask, and stampeded into the scoop. The finger-sized bait, realizing the trap, whirled to escape as Messias lifted the scoop from the water. The fish squirted through the netting, leapt out the top, and in one way or another found their freedom. Reaching into the dwindling mass, Messias grabbed a handful and stuffed them into his mouth, swallowing them whole. A mad race ensued, the bait trying to leave the scoop before he could consume another slithering handful. He managed to swallow three handfuls before the scoop emptied. The few fish that remained were funneled into an unused bootie which was filled with sea water. Before returning to the water he removed the sunshade and laid it across the belly plate. The next load, if there was one, could be dumped and then transferred into booties without incurring such high losses.

The water was as he had left it, bait flying in all directions seeking safety in their numbers. The feeding progressively slowed and within an hour no wahoo were seen. Although maverick schools continued to wander by, the bulk of it had apparently joined up elsewhere. Messias checked the sky to see where the birds were working. Only a few circled and none were diving; the feeding had closed down.

Struggling back onto the boat, Messias re-hung the sunshade and laid beneath it. The bait fish, still quite alive in his stomach, made their attempts to escape and bounced upstream for several seconds before sliding back to their fate. The live meal had done nothing for his thirst. Perhaps even aggravated it with salty scales, and his body felt leached and heavy. To the skies of the southeast, in something akin to a plea, he said, "I need water." It was the first time Messias had made such a request to the stone ear of nature, and it held the measure of his desperation.

The skies remained as mute as they were cloudless. The wind held steady out of the northwest, and instead of trimming the sail, Messias slept.

Later he awoke in lethargy, and made the boat ready in slow-motion movements. Navigating by way of the northwest swells, he occupied himself ferreting out fish scales that had lodged in the crannies of his teeth, ceremoniously spitting the silver flakes into the wind. He sailed into late afternoon, and soon began to nod off at the helm.

The sound of the whale's blow startled him. Their exhales, shooting fifteen foot geysers above barnacled heads, came in explosive bursts of sea mist and whale breath. "Fin whales," shouted Messias with affection, counting five in the pod, "Ho, great fins." Messias had swum with fin whales, as he had swum with grays, and pilots, and orcas, but the fins were very special.

On a sunny afternoon two decades past, while at anchor in a converted shrimp trawler on a bay north of Lorenzo Island in the Sea of Cortez, an adolescent fin whale, forty feet in length, came alongside the boat. The divers and members of the Mexican crew came topside to watch as it laid on its right side looking up at the humans on board. While each species eyed one another, Messias, wearing trunks, a mask and a pair of fins, entered the water and swam to the floating leviathan. At the moment of entry, a rippling spasm shook the body of the whale, and instantly relieved Messias of whatever misgivings he might have had. Reaching out, he stroked the great creature's flesh. Its slick, rubbery skin trembled at his touch, sending a vibration surging unexpectedly up his arm. So strong was the sensation that he could not have pulled away if he had wanted to. The whale's quivering impulses carried into his solar plexus and warmed his chest into expansion. He stroked the full length of the fin whale's body, all the while talking to it in hushed tones. It was said later by those on board that, "it seemed the whale had been instructed to observe and study us, and permitted the same privilege." Messias moved forward to its enormous head, seeking an eye. When contact was made, an indecipherable message was communicated. One that reached across the abyss between whale and man and caused Messias to shake uncontrollably. In the next moment the whale dipped its massive head and sank into the sea.

Messias told no one of the experience, fearing that to speak of it might dilute it and make it less than what it was. Over the years the impact of the meeting abated, yet there remained a bonding thread in the experience that forever linked him to the fin whale. Those same feelings of kinship flooded his chest as the whales disappeared among the swells; their silent voices called across the abyss, and Messias, standing on the belly plate, began to shake.

Sitting back down he heaved a breath unsure if the source of his unsteadiness came from the whales or his weakened condition. The bootie which held the bait fish swung from the aft stay, and he checked it to see if the fish were still alive. All but two had died. He swallowed them one at a time, then repositioned himself at the tiller.

The wind held steady out of the northwest. The boat continued its voyage east, trailing the yellow fishing line. The day-long wind had built a two-foot chop that accompanied deepening swells. The boat bounced along at a knot to a knot and a half. If this wind were to hold for two days and nights, he thought, I could make the coast. But without water I might be too far gone for it to make any difference.

Sailing east and facing west he watched the sun set into a string of low clouds that appeared to have been blown off Mexico's western shore. The clouds created a false horizon for the play of the sun's final rays.

The boat and its helmsman lurched into evening.

The constant movement of the ocean had so thoroughly penetrated Messias that it was difficult to make distinctions between himself and the boat and the ocean. All three merged into a single, rolling swell, pushing its way to Mexico.

Later, the moon rose to his back and reflected off the water. A flying fish arched across the stern, flashing silver moon against the night sky. The moon rose above his head and he remembered McCorkin, and wondered if he would ever find Cynthia to pass on McCorkin's last words. "Why do last words have such clarity that they are able to stop time and forever haunt the present?" he asked the moon.

"Two men broke into a home on Beverly Glen where they murdered and tortured a man and a woman, an apparent drug deal gone sour. It was first believed that they had broken into the wrong house. However, the police are now looking for the daughter of the dead couple who, they have learned, was the girlfriend of a movie producer, and who may have been trying to steal cash and jewelry from her parents in order to buy her way into a stronger position on the film."

Messias flicked off the television set with the remote control. He stared awhile at the blank screen. Such stories no longer horrified him as they once did. He had become numbed by the onslaught and could only manage bewilderment at the madness. Actually he found little difference between what was portrayed as entertainment and what the nightly news offered. Society was a hungry beast that had torn open its stomach and was devouring its own entrails, he numbly observed. He had ceased making attempts to analyze why this was so, for there were too many threads that led back to the source of such misery. It was a plague of monumental proportions. So much more frighteningly because one could view the disembowelment of mankind nightly on television in the sublime comfort of one's home before dozing off to a fitful night's sleep.

Messias reclined back into the lamb skin couch and looked at a crystal unicorn on a glass table that was supported by the tusks of an adolescent elephant. It was surrounded by priceless artifacts from Africa, and porcelain sculptures from China. There were paintings hanging from every wall capturing the full breadth of contemporary art. Yet nothing in this room moved him to inspiration. There was not a single object which could resurrect him from the deadness he felt inside.

The all-pervasive grinding that droned unceasingly in his ears when he first arrived in the city was no longer heard. He had assimilated it as he had the horror stories on television. The splintering of traffic noises were but a dim reminder.

The variety of scents, carried on the wind which he at one time could so precisely identify, where not his to enjoy. Nor, for that matter, could the delicate fragrance of the wind be discerned. The city had overpowered all the delicious smells of nature and had, finally, overpowered itself, leaving but a single carboned odor that dominated the factories and rendered them useless.

He absently rubbed his hands together. They felt smooth and weak. Stretching the muscles in his arms and back, he rose from the couch without tightening his skin, and his flaccid biceps did not stop his forearm from nearly touching his shoulder. He let out a breath and it was short and weak and demanded little of his lungs. He made himself a screwdriver and drank it down in three swallows. He was having glimpses of himself that were not comfortable, and she was not here to distract him, so they fell unimpeded into his consciousness. He exhaled a series of ineffective breaths as if trying to release the demon that had been loosed in his mind.

He rechecked the dinner table to make sure all was in readiness. And even though she was several hours late, as she had been in recent months, he nevertheless took special care in preparing the meals; lobster, scallop in wine and garlic; watercress and green olives stuffed with shrimp, and a fine sauvignon blanc that took nearly all his money. There was smoked cheese, currants in port, and preserved wild cherries. He brought lavender roses and placed them on the table between two candles, lit at the hour of her expected arrival.

But she did not come, and he left the table, the candles burning, her glass filled, his glass empty, and went into the night.

It was a short walk to the well lit, well policed, tree lined, swept shopping center cleanly called "the Village." Here college kids and the upwardly mobile brought their women to ten dollar movies and four dollar ice cream cones. They wore hundred dollar sneakers, and five hundred dollar leather jackets and their tee shirts expounded four word philosophies. They arrived in cars that were made in Germany no less than three years ago, the cost of which would feed a village of thirty in Biafra everyday for twenty years.

Messias sat on a clean wooden bench and watched this laughing, carefree world indulge itself. Their smiles spoke of lives without hardship or loss, without courage or curiosity, and without generosity or soul. Messias was ignored on his bench as if he were invisible. He wouldn't have been surprised if a couple had absently sat on him. They saw nothing but reflections of themselves in the polished fenders of their cars; in the display windows of the expensive stores; in the actors on the movie screen; and in each other. Their lives could get no better, nor any worse. He was as empty as their smiles, and as devoid of himself as they were of substance.

He thought about the sea and the spontaneity of the ocean wilderness and its moment to moment unpredictability that had once lifted his senses to their peak of awareness. He longed for the smells and the force of the wind and currents. The struggle to simply survive. He longed to seek the face of the Great Spirit again in all things natural. He rose from the bench and hurried home.

The candles had burned to their ends and left hardened pools of white wax upon the table. She had returned home, but the food had remained untouched.

"I waited for you then left," said Messias.

As cool as the wax, she replied, "There was business to attend to. You know, business. That thing we all do for money, so we might have the necessities of life."

"I'm not afraid of hard work," he said gently.

"You can't hold down a job for longer than three months. How could you possibly know what hard work really is?"

He waited before replying, attempting to hold back the words, but they came tumbling out from the force of being held in check for too long. "I don't belong here. I belong on the ocean, inside the sea. I don't recognize my own voice. I've got to get back..."

"I hate to break it to you," she interrupted, "but this is not the ocean. This is the real world."

He replied softly, "there's not a shred of realness in this world."

"Does that include me?" she asked in a detached way that filled him with a terrible wonder, like the onset of madness.

"I love you," was all he said.

"Love isn't enough," she replied, her green eyes narrowing like a cat that has eyed a bird. "Not nearly enough. You've gone through six jobs in two years. You haven't worked in eight months. I'm embarrassed to take you to cocktail parties. I don't bring you to gallery openings because you can't carry on a decent conversation with anyone but the custodian."

Messias remained silent for a long moment, staring down at her face framed in perfection on the white satin pillow.

"I've looked at you for too long. I can't defend myself. Come, live with me in the ocean."

She sighed a faraway breath, and pondered a thought for a moment as though it were smoke blown from a cigarette. "I've been having an affair," she finally said. "Now do you want to defend yourself? At least get angry, for Christ sakes!"

Messias imperceptibly flinched. The inside of his chest exploded into shattered glass. He did not utter a word.

He should have left that night. But he did not leave for three months because he couldn't. There were days when he would marvel at the pain in his heart. It was as tangible as the rain and it spilled into his stomach and made him sick. On other days the full mystery of love consumed him. How, he asked, could the simple glance of another bring such overwhelming joy and then such crushing pain? What is it inside my head that so affects my heart and turns me worthless?

She became more detached as the weeks wore on, and he fell deeper into the unhealable wound in his heart.

When he left her he also left the United States. He wandered into Mexico where the faces of the people were as maskless as the creatures of the sea.

But the creatures of the sea could not love, nor could they keep out the loneliness. Messias continued to see her face, and remembered her as a dream that was held for a passing moment. Now his life laid bare as one long dream in which he, for the most part, had sleep-walked through as both the dreamer and the dreamed.

Balancing on the willowy edge of death, there was no room for false dreams or illusions. All men who have had time to die know this, (although few acknowledge it). The dreams of day, thought Messias, were created to divert ones attention from the harsh truths of existence. In that, the ocean has saved me from living my entire life as a dream; it's the place where dream and illusion can't exist. It's the only reality I ever believed in.

Messias' legs had slipped from the aft buoy, and hung lifelessly in the water. Fatigue had caught him and bludgeoned him into sleep; his head rolled like a drunk's, and he slept the sleep of the dead.

❖ 12 ❖

THREE PELICANS FLOATED IN A LAVENDER SKY. Messias followed their flight, running a swollen tongue over cracked lips. The edges of his throat met in a dry swallow. Gingerly, he shifted to his knees, and faced the well of the wet suit, where scarcely a teaspoon had collected. The wind that drove the boat during the night had consumed its share of sea dew. Drops were taken, held in the mouth, and absorbed into tissues, leaving but a trickle for the throat. The sail held scattered droplets, and he found a covey under an arm out of the wind. Licking them clean, his tongue scraped like sand paper over the neoprene. Working his way to a standing position, he surveyed the horizon. An object resembling a mast trembled to the south, but the distance prevented a clear identification.

The wind, which had been steady for eighteen hours, continued to blow and he settled into place, pointing for the rising sun. The sail protected him from its early rays, but later the shade was lashed to the aft stay to cover his head and upper body. It deflected the wind and boat speed was lost. There was no choice; lengthy exposure in the direct sun would have ravaged him.

Near noon a school of dolphin converged on the craft leaping about in friendly greeting. Messias smiled back at the dolphin, "Am I getting close to land?" Through the years he had made attempts to establish contact with dolphin. Several times he had jumped into their midst from a boat, and swum out from shore to intercept them as they cut through a surf line. They had always kept their distance, and moved no closer than was prudent. Messias understood; he had heard the cries of harpooned dolphin. If he were a dolphin, he would not trust man either. Despite their caution, he felt a natural kinship with the dolphin. Where the whale seemed superior and aloof, the dolphin, in their cheery playfulness, evoked a sense of fraternity.

Messias always smiled when dolphins appeared. He couldn't help it. It was doubtful that the three dolphin who had driven off the shark and had reappeared when McCorkin died were of this school. This one was heading south, and though they meandered as they passed the boat, they kept to their course. A half hour elapsed before the last had swum by and disappeared into sea chop.

The thin string of clouds that appeared in last night's sunset had since acquired bulk, giving circumstantial evidence that a front might be building in the southeast. Near mid-afternoon a southerly shift in the wind further supported the notion. Messias's hopes didn't lift so much as did his state of alertness, which had slipped considerably with his physical decline. Adjusting the sail to the wind shift, he sailed for an hour, then stood to check for boats that might have slid in behind the three-foot swells. Rising on rubbery legs, he lost footing to the gyrating seas, grabbed the aft stay to break his fall, then released it for fear of capsizing the leaning boat. Laughing, he fell into the sea.

The light craft, without his weight, jumped ahead in the wind. Seeing the potential for disaster, he immediately set out after it. Arms stiff from non-use, and legs without swim fins labored in the water. The southerly was pushing the boat downwind, and after a half minute swim, Messias stopped to catch his breath. Treading water in the rolling seas he caught sight of it on a cresting up-swell fifty feet away.

Generally, a sailboat's inclination is to turn into the wind and heave. This makeshift craft did not respond to those tendencies and continued to run with the gusting wind.

Messias buried his face in the water and set out after the boat. Within minutes arm and leg movement were reduced to near floundering, and he was forced to stop again and recapture his breath. Bobbing on an up-swell thirty feet away, the boat had made its turn and was facing into the southerly. It danced in and out of its tracks as the wind caught it at the top of swells. Knowing that this next effort could be his last, he dug into the chop with abandon. Arms flailing, and legs nearly dead, he closed the distance to twenty feet, then ten. A gust drove the boat over an oncoming swell and out of reach. In a final, desperate effort, he lunged for it. Physical resources expended, he fought the water with his will, but was unable to swim another stroke.

In that narrow space that lies between the moment of defeat, and the moment of surrender, a thin yellow line appeared six feet beneath him. Bending, he snatched the fishing line that trailed behind the boat, and carefully, so as not to release the slip not, pulled it to him. Clutching the aft buoy when it was within reach, he lay his head against the neoprene and floated limp in the water. When he attempted to climb back into the boat he hadn't the strength to lift himself above the ribs, so tipped the boat and rolled into it. In the maneuver his trunks caught a rib and tore, and he pushed his hand through the sheet of the sailfish skin that covered the bottom. He laid stilled on the belly plate afraid to feel the totality of his exhaustion.

When he regained himself, he inched his way to a sitting position, and with weighted arms trimmed the sail and fixed the tiller between legs that trembled. The turbulent seas further punished him, and his will went the way of his limbs.

In the late afternoon he gathered himself to stand for a watch. Looping a safety line around a shoulder and under the opposite arm, he staggered to his feet. Reaching full height he immediately saw a ketch, three miles due south, heading northwest. Cautiously kneeling back down and adjusting the sail, he altered course to intercept. The swell came from the northwest, impeding progress, but the wind was right. A half hour into the new heading, it was obvious that the ketch could not be intercepted. "If I'd seen it earlier," he said aloud. "I forgot to stand. No, I was too tired, and too afraid." The ketch, less than two miles away, cut cleanly through the water making good time in the southerly. He watched until it was consumed by white-lipped swells.

The setting sun flared the sky mandarin orange. Messias's tongue, as rough as a pumice stone, worked the inside of his mouth much as a baby works its mother's nipple. There was no point in trying to eat turtle if none could be swallowed. The sun reflected off the deepening clouds in soft oranges trimmed in veins of gold. There were signs of a storm brewing all right, but without the accompanying mares tails that normally define tropical storms, he held doubts. If doubts were flagons of water, he would be in no need of a storm. He doubted he possessed the necessary strength to handle another turtle. He doubted there was enough moisture in the flesh of a fish to turn back the dehydration that had set in, or that he had sufficient means to capture a fish, if indeed it could fill his needs.

The sunset grew to spectacular proportions. The low clouds lent depth to a canvas on which laser strokes of radiant reds and vivid golds had been blazed for their solitary showing. Messias was not witness to natures art work. Having broken free from the bonds of the belly plate, he soared with the untroubled gulls and stately pelicans in their passage to eastern landfall. As the last light struck a thin golden line the length of the recumbent clouds, he returned from his open-eyed travels and pulled the sunshade down, loosely covering himself against the chill.

The boat rocks twenty feet away, and having no idea how he has fallen in the water, he sluggishly swims for it. Arms and legs heavy, it is difficult for him to gain the boat. There is no wind, and the boat isn't sailing. Perhaps a current is running. Boring down with purposeful strokes, his breaths come in gasps. The water feels as mud and he pauses for another look, expecting to have closed the distance, but there is a considerable way to swim yet. Strokes become flails and strength ebbs from his body as water drains from a sink. Reflexively he stops swimming when his leg makes contact with a solid object. Without a face mask it is not difficult to see the phosphorescent torpedoes turning in quick, edgy movements below. The fear he is holding cracks and breaks like a child's gutter-built dam, and his terror spews into the water. The sharks rise to the smell of terror. Punching away the first with a bare fist, he whirls to kick off another that comes from behind. Two more circle, then rush, turning before contact is made. Swirling phosphorescence fills the blackness. Giving a look in the direction of the boat, it is not where it is supposed to be. A shark noses his stomach, and is pushed away with both hands. Again he searches for the boat, and sees it rocking ten feet away. A shark zips in from behind and is kicked. It snaps at the foot, tearing a piece of meat from the heel. Black blood erupts from the wound as he swims wildly for the boat. The sharks move to the thrashing line of blood. Grasping the boat with one hand, he fends off a shark with the other, feeling its teeth ripping flesh. Blood gushes into the sea. Stricken and clinging to the aft float, he feels a pressure on his hip. A shark has bitten into his torso. Frantically, he beats at its head with fists, and gouges at its eyes and then is jerked beneath the surface.

Lying in the center of the boat with the wet suit covering him, Messias' heart pounded in time to foreshortened breaths. If any fluid had been available, it would have flushed out through open pores. Transfixed, he blinked at a piece of moon that was all but obscured by cloud cover. Then, as if moving from one dream to another, it began to drizzle rain. Still possessed by the night-marish shark dream, he didn't immediately respond to the rain. The drops turned heavy and stirred him into movement. Releasing the base of the wet suit, he held it to the sky with both hands. The down pour was brief, turning to drizzle, then to a fine mist, then ceasing altogether. The front, what there was of it, passed without yielding another drop. The hood well collected half a cup of rain water, and he dipped a hand into the sea and mixed it with the fresh water. Drinking half the contents, he emptied the rest into the bootie that had been lined with the stomach of the turtle. Licking the sail of rain drops, he reclined back on the belly plate and the terror of the shark dream returned in sickly waves.

Messias was not interested in sleep, and waited for rain, and watched the moon dip in and out of the fleeing cloud cover. Also he eyed the water for triangled fins; neither the rain nor the sharks came again.

❖ 13 ❖

THE SUN FORETOLD THE FUTURE in its wincing pain of reflected light. From the hood, Messias drank a tablespoon of water that had accumulated, then lifted the water bootie and sipped a small swallow. Less than half of the reserve was left—three swallows. Sitting back down on the belly plate with a piece of turtle jerky, he bit into the leather-like strip, but there was not enough moisture in his mouth to break down the stringy meat, so he dipped it into the ocean to soften. He swung his legs in the water between the ribs of the boat to work away their stiffness. He also stretched the muscles in his shoulders and back. In between stretches and swings, he managed to down half a stick of jerky.

Draping a line over a shoulder, he rose unsteadily to a standing position. The lively ocean had him holding to the bill of the sailfish. The undulating blue gave no sign of life, its emptiness rivaled that of the water bootie. A twelve-knot wind was blowing the last of the clouds northward, and would be losing velocity soon. Squatting back down on the belly plate he adjusted the sail and pointed the boat into the white eye of the sun. A mile into the sail the slip knot on the yellow fishing line snapped free and whipped out into the sea. Grabbing it, he put pressure on the line with thumb and forefinger. The line zipped through the pressure, cutting into his thumb, drawing blood. A large dorado broke water, flashing its rainbow colors. The fish ran out all one hundred feet of line, and Messias scarcely had time to wrap its end around his hand and brace himself. The line shivered, pulling the bent arm straight, and snapped. Unwrapping it from his fist, he tossed it into the water, and repositioned himself on the belly plate. He resumed sailing without giving the dorado, the hook, or the line another thought.

The southerly died a slow death, succumbing near noon, and Messias tied off the tiller when the boat could not maintain a course, and fell asleep beneath the sunshade. He awoke to find a large shark, wide and thick, and light brown—the color of applesauce—circling the boat. It cut beneath the boat and slid under the aft buoy, nicking it with its dorsal fin and resurrected the dream of last night. The shark stayed with the boat making wide circles around its perimeter. Messias stared at a bead of light that blinked from the tip of its dorsal fin. After awhile the single point of light commingled with the glittering sea, and the shark was forgotten.

The wind swirled in directionless eddies, which the boat traced in slick patterns on the surface. Lost in trance, Messias failed to see three dolphin jump outside the circling shark and extinguish its bead of light. The sound of an exhale brought his head around and his vacant face bent into a smile when three dolphin swam next to the boat. "You have chased off the shark," he said. "While you're at it, grab a line and tow me to the nearest shore." And he tossed a line into the water. It floated untouched to starboard. "Go on, take it. I have a firm grip."

The dolphins did not take the line. They smiled, as always, but they did not take the line. Messias left it floating on the surface. The dolphins swam around the boat, rolling to one side, then the other, their one eye breaking the surface. Returning their gaze, he felt himself on the stringers of a familiar bridge; an invitation to cross had been extended. The dolphins lifted their heads from the water, held them high for a moment, then dipped back in and swam off to the southeast.

Messias was certain that these were the same three that were with him the night McCorkin had died, and who earlier had driven off the shark. He remembered McCorkin's strained uttering that these dolphin would protect them until they were found. Dismissing it at the time, he now felt a sense of security in the dolphin's presence and wanted them to return. He waited into late afternoon, but they did not come back.

As if possessed, he blurted out, "I must make another hook!" He pulled the knife from its sheath and the gill plate from beneath the foul smelling sailfish. Setting forward on the belly plate with the gill plate between spread legs, he began to scratch out a hook. Instead of using the sharp knife of McCorkin's, he used the one that had been dulled by the cutting of the last hook and the butchering of the turtle. The knife slipped on the first go around and nearly sliced into his leg. On the third pass it wrenched loose from his hand, and in fumbling for it, he knocked it into the water. Bending to the surface, he watched it sink, then leaned back and disgustedly announced, "You will kill yourself before the ocean has a chance! You've become dull and useless like the knife. Maybe you should follow it to the depths and be done with it."

Tilting his head back until it rested on the swim fin that leaned against the sailfish, he stretched his legs their full length and let them dangle in the water to the calf. The sun fell full across his face, and he dozed in its radiance.

Messias slept and a white bird circled the boat. It hovered, then landed on the aft stay that supported the sunshade. Awakened by the sound of the wind in its wings, he squinted into the sun saying, "What kind of bird is this? Have you brought me a message? Are you resting from a long journey?"

The finely-sculptured gull shone brilliantly, its white breast cut like stone, its wings like delicate, albino hands, folded across themselves sheltering the tail. It cocked its head, and studied Messias with its left eye, then with both eyes. Straight on it had the intense look of an eagle, with a sharp, low, brow rising from its yellow bill. Its gaze, thought Messias, was enough to turn any bait belly up. Reaching for a stick of turtle jerky, and twisting off a small piece, he threw it into the air. The gull snatched it out of the sky, and swallowed it in the same motion.

One eye closed to the sun, Messias said, "I am dying. I think you already know that. Have you come to carry my soul to the heavens? Or are you here to peck out my eyes?"

The gull stared unblinking.

"Are you what I'm to become in my next life? Will I assume your body? That wouldn't be so bad. Gulls are similar to humans: beautiful, blessed with a certain grace, yet obnoxious and greedy, easily given to hysteria. It should be an easy transition."

The white bird cocked its head, its eye on the jerky.

Messias tore off another piece, and threw it into the air. The bird snatched it as before. He fed the bird the turtle strip, piece by piece, until it was gone. "That is all you'll get white bird. I have problems of my own." The bird remained on the aft stay, and Messias closed his eyes. Later he awoke, and in reaching for the water bootie startled it into flight. "I have so little water," he said aloud. "What's it matter if I drink it all now or four hours from now? There's not enough to save me. It'll only prolong my misery." But he did not drink from the bootie and returned it to its place.

The overhead sun was squeezing him. It would be better, he thought, for me to be in the water. Looping a line over a shoulder, and with the face mask and snorkel on, he wondered out loud if the shark had returned, or if the dolphins had chased it all the way to Cerralvo. Realizing that he had been speaking aloud to himself for most of the day, he pulled the snorkel from his mouth and said through a grin, "This must be what happens when you die alone," then reinserted it and slipped into the water.

He laid spread eagle on the surface, surrendering to the steady rhythm of the light swells. The ocean absorbed his pain as a poultice draws puss from a wound. Drifting free from the gravity of the physical world he floated as a cloud upon the ceiling of another sky.

In the ocean's diamond clarity, minute particles, like translucent dust, passed before him. Drawn into sharp focus, the particles were neither dust, nor debris, but life. Some wiggled along, others pulsated to a steady beat, still others drifted as on a wind. A single, delicate organism that first appeared as a kind of membrane, strayed in front of his face mask. It resembled a pin feather that might have fallen from an exotic hummingbird. A bubble, at the base of its stem, no larger than a grain of Caribbean sand, kept the feather afloat. The delicate ribs of the feather undulated in unbroken rhythm, giving the impression that the organism was destination bound. Messias marveled at its steadfast, lonely journey, one that seemed as aimless as the flight of a dandelion seed caught in a prairie wind. Despite the currents and wild seas that truly determined its course, this ocean seed proceeded as if its destiny were well in hand; as if existence had value; as if arrival was awaited; as if life had meaning. In this minute, transparent seed, Messias saw himself.

The mesmeric journey of the seed pulled Messias into its pulsation's, and the ocean life transformed to glittery dust suspended in a windless, blue room. The liquid ocean ceased to exist. As he breathed, so did all that was suspended. From the sparkling transparency materialized a great silver fish. It approached slowly, circled once then hovered at arms length. It vibrated in a blue/white light, a wingless creature amongst star-bright particles. Messias went to it and extended his hand. It absorbed his hand, and then his arm, finally his body merged with the great fish. As one they dove to depth, splattering the cyanic sky. The ocean rushed into his mouth and out his gills, its oxygen, pure as mountain water, flowed into his heart, and wandered down the length of his lateral line. The vibrations of a thousand galaxies were received, and the ocean swelled with the volume of its voices. A single language was understood.

The depths turned dark and the pressure mounted. Plummeting into the blackness, the surface voices receded and from the depths a distant humming was perceived. In the lightless void the pressure increased and compressed the fish/man to an ocean seed. Then to nothing. From the nothingness came the cry of the fin whale. In a single swelling harmony it carried him across the broad expanse of an inner sea. Reaching a far and liquid shore the darkness held a presence that was all the more felt because it could not be seen. It pierced Messias with its ocean secrets; secrets he had always carried, but had not known. Secrets he had felt, but could not touch. There came a rushing together of the two worlds, both in perfect unison; his spirit with the Great Spirit; his face the face of the Great Spirit.

In tranquil union he heard a voice calling his name from afar. The voice was his own and it pulled him as though it were a magnet and he an iron filing floating in a sea of fire tipped particles. Slowly at first, then accelerating to a blinding speed, he burst through a panel of white light, and re-entered his body. Shocked by the cold and discomfort of the physical world, he struggled to regain the belly plate, and ripped away the last of his trunks on a fish spine. The wound drew blood and its pain completed his return.

Under the sunshade, he relived the experience as one might a dream, except it was not a dream. There was nothing vague or abstract about it. All was understood, and while the source of this understanding was unclear, its truth was undeniable.

The sun dropped into the sea like a stone. Bouquets of cumulus glowed orange then pink and moved at a brisk pace. The sea shook with confusion and birds vibrated between the clouds, the horizon, and the jumping sea. Messias followed the flight of seven golden birds streaking for the coast, their wings on fire, thermal contrails stretching across a saffron sky. Hallucination and reality intermingled and were impossible to differentiate. A panorama of brilliant golds, reds and oranges swirled about, leaving the ocean to temper the last rays of the sun to opalescent steam.

Messias lifted the water bootie and slipped a swallow, then covered himself with the sunshade. The star-lit sky mirrored the phosphorescent ocean and he laid suspended amidst the sparkling universes, certain he floated in the center of it all.

❖ 14 ❖

LOW CLOUDS HUNG OFF OF MEXICO'S western shore and made for a gray dawn. The sea glinted of burnished steel. A jack crevalle broke water, and rivulets of solder ran from its tail. The ocean turned silver and an albatross suspended above, oscillating in a stainless sky. Messias worked his way to a sitting position and bowed to the hood. Its offering, received and held, bathed a swollen tongue. Rising to his knees he licked the sail, and only by their absence did he know the drops were consumed.

In the sunless dawn he shook with chill and recovered himself. The sun finally broke from the clouds and its warmth brought a small pleasure. The boat drifted aimlessly in the placid air. Elongated swells held him momentarily airborne, then gently lowered him into a shallow valley of blue. The easy, rhythmic, rising and falling had a soothing effect, not unlike the movement in the womb when a mother walks. Messias fell into dreamless sleep.

He awoke with head aching. The cool water beckoned. His reason, having twisted in the sun, softened his judgement, and he lay in indecision. The rapacious sun drove him finally from the belly plate, and putting on mask and snorkel and looping a line over a shoulder, he tumbled overboard.

Gazing deep into the cool blue leagues where flickering shafts of sunlight disappeared, there came a sudden urge to follow them down; to kick beyond neutral buoyancy and let the weight of the water carry the momentum, arms, like wings spread, descending from another sky back into the dense atmosphere of his birthing. Soaring in that inevitable and final flight, winging his way to the consumation of all freedoms.

Messias did not fly, could not fly. Floating on the surface, he drifted between two skies, rising and falling in that unbound world of the dying.

Lingering before the seamouth of mortality, a silver and white image appeared. It had the sharp, contrasting markings of a bird, and it entered his field of vision where effervescent blue had been a moment before, then vanished. Unknowing, he blinked, and the form appeared again. A dolphin glided closely by, inspecting with a clear eye.

Messias looked into the eye and lost himself in its dark warmth. The dolphin rose to the surface, exhaled, then swam down to join two dolphin circling below. He wished to dive and greet them, but a feeble kick was all he could muster, and he bobbed weakly on the surface. The nearest dolphin swam to within several feet, and Messias extended his hand. The dolphin banked out of reach, surfaced for a breath, and came back, defecating in front of him. The emission broke into an expanding cloud of particles. What does it want? He thought, should I do the same? I've nothing to crap out. Reaching for the cloud of dolphin feces, he closed his hand around it. At the gesture, the two from below accelerated to the surface, broke water, and leapt into the air. The third dolphin swam slowly back and forth an arms length away, and Messias felt a wave of warmth pass through him, then the three dolphin formed up and sped off into aqua marine space.

A profound loneliness overcame Messias. Dry sobs choked his throat, empty tear ducts opened and spilled their dust on his cheeks. Floating on the surface he hoped that the dolphins would return. He waited until he shook with cold, and when he could stand no more pulled the boat to him and rolled into it, the fish spines stabbing at him.

A glowing red ball balanced atop a thread that was the horizon. A long-billed egret glided above, eyed the boat, circled once, and turned east. The sun, having slipped beneath the protection of the sunshade, was beating directly on him and was of no consequence. The survival instincts that had carried him to within sight of landfall could not respond to the call.

Broken cumulus shimmered on the horizon. Rays of golden light from the partially ellipsed sun pierced the reddening sky like beacons, forewarning of shoal-strewn, uncharted territory. Messias, aware that this sunset would be his last, waited until the final pastel cloud turned gray, then pushed his way to a sitting position. Paddling the boat so it faced east he untied the water bootie from the aft stay, and took a piece of turtle jerky from the container. It was not for nourishment that he was about to partake of this meal. Dipping the meat into the ocean to soften, he nibbled off a piece and followed it with a sip of water. Messias was entering into his death, and it was in this communion that he ate and drank until the water was gone. Reaching into the sea, he lifted a handful of water and spilled it across his face, then laid down, partially covering himself with the wet suit top.

The first evening star shone low and ineffable on the horizon. Others soon clustered about it and the sky filled with their light. The sound of an exhaled breath broke across the sea sounds.

Three dolphin gleamed in starlight off the port beam.

Messias extended his hand and agitated the water. One of the dolphin glided to it in a snowy shower of phosphorescence. Rising under the hand, it made contact with the man. Messias stroked its smooth head, "If you have come to save me, you're too late," he said.

The dolphin submerged and released a large bubble.

"I'm glad you're here. Please stay."

The dolphins stayed with the boat, and the noise of their exhales consoled him. Their companionship was a natural thing and he continued to speak to them. "I've done much in my life. Many things few men have experienced. Yet, I've missed the mark. I've been moving in the same circle.

A break of water. A misty exhale.

"Maybe I didn't know where to look, or how to look. When I was very young, I knew. You know where to look, don't you?"

The slick body glistened in starlight, rising and falling in the low swells.

"Tell me dolphin, before I die, in what direction must I look? A great something has been missed. There is emptiness in me where I should be full."

The dolphin exhaled. Its breath reached the nostrils of Messias and entered him.

"Nourish me dolphin. Feed me what I need."

Rippled sea parted. A curved line rose, glinted, then disappeared.

"You can't feed me, can you? No one can feed another. My mistake was a lack of boldness when I knew the truth. Now it's too late. I've taken in all that I can, and I'm left with a hunger."

The dolphin rolled on its side, its eye bright with intelligence.

A wave arched, then crashed. Messias fell silent, listening to his inner sounds.

A breeze freshened out of nowhere, then faded.

The moon rose out of the swells in the east and reflected brightly on the backs of the dolphin when they broke water for a breath.

Messias shivered uncontrollably, ignoring the chill until it became unfelt.

The three dolphin stayed with the man through the night.

❖ 15 ❖

HE HAS BEEN WATCHING THE MIRROR LAKE from atop a lofty branch of a withered and leafless tree. Its perfect circle accentuating the place where it has broken, and where the water spills steadily away; running over rock and granite, down empty gullies and canyons, across petrified forests and into barren flatlands, where it settles and disappears into the cracks of the earth, turning the dust into mud.

There comes an urgency to leave this place that for so long has been home. Lifting from the tree, a broken wing forces him to fly in tight circles, gaining altitude around the circumference of the lake. He climbs until the highest peaks of the tallest mountains are at eye level. He climbs into the clouds, dark and heavy with moisture and travels to their core. A lightness comes, and the one wing folds into his body and he vaporizes into the mist of the cloud, stretching formless from horizon to horizon.

Free from gravity and the hardship of earthly existence, he floats in peaceful serenity.

Yet the earth will not leave him. Its essence lies in the moisture which carries its scent, and it beckons in anguished pleas.

"Nourish me", comes the cry of the earth in warming breaths. The cloud that is him shakes at its touch, and rumbles with uncertainty. From horizon to horizon he trembles and is released and falls to earth. Striking its skin, he is absorbed into its tissues. Roots of plants and trees voraciously receive him. Dormant seeds lying in wait quake into birthing. He courses through the veins of branches and into leaves, and up the stems of flowers whose perfumed petals open to the sun. He washes the dust from stones and fills the lakes. He sends the streams and rivers to running and the mouse and deer to drinking. The eagle tips its beak to him and the serpent wets its tongue. The lion and the ram, the ant and the opossum take him in, and he knows them all. He falls across the mountain ranges and plains, and across the desert, and on every ocean and sea. He nourishes the earth, and all that lives upon her is known to him.

❖ 16 ❖

THE DOLPHINS LEFT BEFORE DAY BREAK. Messias had no knowledge of their departure. In semiconsciousness he laid upon the belly plate. The dream had opened the final flood gate.

From a copper sky the sun came, and the first delicious rays that follow a chilling night were lost on him. The sun rose and he did not move. The wet suit top had been cast off, and he lay naked to the sun. Terns, frigates and pelicans crisscrossed high in a cornflower sky.

Near mid-morning, in a final voluntary act, he rolled from the belly plate into the sea, brown stomach turned to the blue sky. Throughout the morning he lapsed in and out of consciousness and did not feel the sun's heat nor the water's coolness.

The sun reached its summit and began its descent, rendering him into delirium. Ships of fire sailed on seas of white ice. Voices called his name. Golden dolphins with emerald eyes soared over black mountain tops where stood a pale stallion in waiting. The light dimmed and brilliant colors illuminated ancient Indian temples. The image of himself was vaguely perceived, floating in a white pool.

The three dolphin returned and circled him, listening to the incoherent ramblings.

Shadow enveloped him and the fire in his brain had very nearly burnt out. He saw his body floating on the water, and the three dolphin triangularly enclosing it.

From a deep cavern came a light, bright and very white, pleasant and warm, and he moved toward it. It receded and a voice echoing distantly says, "do not leave." The voice is gentle, very much like his own voice, but not entirely.

The image of his body fades.

The bright light comes again in a rush of brilliance. Beyond it lies his brown and bearded form floating in the gentle swell.

A voice from inside says, "Stay outside the body."

The naked form assumes a sharpness. He sees the three dolphin lolling beside it.

The voice, stronger than before, says, "Stay outside the body. It is safe."

The voice is reassuring and reflects a sense of peacefulness. He thinks, "I will stay", and his position above the body acquires stability.

"We wait for you," says the voice in his head.

"Who are you?" he thinks.

"We are of the Mother; you call us dolphins."

"Is this death?" thinks Messias.

"Your body is alive," says the voice.

"Is this a dream?"

"Dreams are always a possibility," says the voice.

"How am I able to communicate with you?" thinks Messias.

"You are beyond your body," instructs the voice. "The channel is open."

"I hear you in the back of my head. Is this some kind of telepathy?"

"It is what you call it."

"What's going on? Why are you here?"

"We have been waiting. The Ancient One said that an Intercessor would come. It is you."

"What's an Intercessor?" asks Messias.

"It will be explained."

"Have you been with me this entire time?"

"When you called, we came."

"Is this how dolphins communicate, telepathically?"

"It is not necessary."

"What is it to be a dolphin?"

"We are alive," comes the voice in Messias head. "We live. The gift is given. We sing, eat, love, join, give birth, merge, dream and teach our young. You also have the gift."

"It is not the same," says Messias. There was a long silence after his response, and he feared that contact might have broken, so asks, "What do you teach your young?"

"All things must be taught. Only eating, play and sleep come naturally."

"What do you sing?"

"We sing our song. Every creature has their song. It describes to the Family who they are."

"Do I have a song?"

"The Ancient One says that you have lost your song and cannot hear the song of the Mother and the Father."

"Who are the Mother and the Father?"

"The Mother bears us. She provides. She lives in us and we are an extension of Her. She is an extension of us. We flow in the seven directions. We are Her children. She is the source of all that lives."

"Who is the Father?"

"You are of the Father. You do not know this?"

"Yes, I know," says Messias realizing the Father. "How do you communicate?"

"There is no need. All is known."

"What do you mean?"

"Our sound sees all emotion, all dis-ease. It has no boundaries. It dwells in unfilled space. We cannot hide from the sounds of those in our tribe. We have nothing to hide from. We sing of ourselves openly. We are of each other. We are of the tribe. We are of the Family."

"Are you also of me?" Messias asks.

"You are of the Family. We are of you. We have entered you, and know of your dis-ease."

"Could I feel you when you entered me?"

"In merging the other feels."

"Is merging like sex? Is it intercourse?"

"That is joining."

"Can you merge into me?"

A faint murmur comes from beneath Messias's heart. A tingling sensation spreads to his stomach and chest. It increases in volume until his entire body vibrates with a sound; not so much a sound that is heard, more one that is felt. It penetrates into dry, abandoned cracks of held pain, and flows into crevices cleaved from loss and frustration. It fills the hollow places as an incoming tide washes into basins of an exposed reef. It sweeps away barriers that have taken a lifetime to erect. The song of the dolphin plays in Messias and he surrenders to its sympathetic chords. Reaching a crescendo, it sustains until he feels he will shatter from the vibrations.

The song descends in tremolo and meter, leaving him reverberating in its undertone. A warmth spreads thinly from his abdomen and enters that which was cleansed by the song. The loneliness that had eroded out its trenches in Messias is flooded with the dolphins' love, and the source of his hunger is known. The gentle voice asks, "Do you hear your song?"

In deep recognition, Messias bathes in its mellifluent tones.

Messias is aroused from his halcyon state by a fathomless sound that comes from all directions at once. A might geyser shoots forty feet into the air and beneath it a fin whale surfaces. A voice speaks in the similar way of the dolphin, but is heard near the chest, rather than in the head. "We have been waiting for you," it says.

Messias asks, "Am I the first human to hear your voice?"

"You are not the first," comes the voice in his chest. "You're the last."

"I don't understand."

"Your understanding of the nature of things is limited. There have been others. Once, all tribes belonged to the Family of the Mother and the Father. We shared in the gifts. We communicated. All knew their song and the song of every tribe."

"What happened?"

"Your species gained the superior position across the Father. You became the master weapons maker and eliminated all tribes different than yourselves. Your song became scattered and your meaning for existence lost. You are of the Mother and of the Father, but you stand outside of them. We waited, believing you would eliminate yourselves as similar tribes had done before. This nearly occurred, but in your salvation, you gained the means to destroy all of life. Since that most recent occurrence, our attempts to contact you have failed."

"There was no awareness of your efforts."

"We have sent emissaries who were willing to sacrifice their freedom so that we might communicate as you and I are now. In the arrogance of your species, it was believed the sounds we made were a form of speech. You attempted to manipulate us to suit your conceptions, and were unwilling to experiment with yourselves. The bridge of communication lay in a change within you. As it must now be clear, our methods of communication have developed far beyond your primitive modes. It is forgotten that we had reached complete physical evolvement millions of years before your species walked upright. The sounds we make are not for speech. They serve a more meaningful purpose. Our tongues are incapable of speech as you practice it. It would be as impossible for us to develop a physical method of communication as it would for you to reacquire the gills you once had."

"How is it that you know so much about us?"

"We carry your history from its beginnings, as we carry the history of every tribe that has lived, and those which no longer exist."

"We have slaughtered your species shamelessly," thought Messias. "Why, with your superior intelligence, are we able to so easily kill you—your tribe?"

"We have freely traveled this sphere for fifty million years. Our physical construction limited our explorations. As you are beginning to explore the Mother, we sought to know the Father, and as you now rest outside your body, so we developed the ability to voluntarily leave our bodies. Once free of our confinement we traveled the Father, and discovered His extraordinary beauty. We dwelled on His mountains, and wandered among His forests. We know of His lakes and rivers, and have seen His creatures and inhaled His flowers. We have visited your cities, sat with you while you ate, made love, worked, built and destroyed. We are in awe of your capacity for suffering. In this recent time of ships we became your prey. We are easy to hunt because we are rarely in our bodies. By the time your harpoons are buried into our flesh, it is too late. Only during mating and the rearing of our young are we within our bodies."

"Can dolphins also leave their bodies?"

"The dolphins possess that same ability, but their joy is in movement. They are dancers, and their's is a celebration unfettered by curiosity."

"Still, they are killed in our nets."

"Dolphins have lived upon this planet without natural enemies. In their play your violence and nets are the last thing they expect. That same violence is destroying the Mother and the Father. This is why you have been summoned. You are the messenger — the Intercessor. You have become the final hope for the Mother and the Father."

"The final hope? What do you mean?"

"We have attempted to communicate with others of your tribe. Their fear of the Mother causes them to surrender, and accelerates their death. You are of the Mother as well as the Father. The fear does not exist in you. The channels are open."

"What is it you want me to do?"

"We ask that you intercede in our behalf, that you speak for all who cannot be heard. Your tribe has become a disease that has spread across the Father and penetrated the Mother. Both will perish at your hands. We ask that you return to the Father and your tribe and bring an end to this destruction."

"No one will listen to me. I am insignificant."

"You shall have the power you need."

"I don't think you understand. The power I need is in the hands of those who are poisoning the earth. They won't give it up."

"We have observed your tribe from its inception. Our understanding of it is complete. On the second full moon from this one, every dolphin and whale in every sea and ocean on the sphere will gather off the shores of your coastal cities. When the sun is at its highest, they will simultaneously leap from the water. You will predict this event. When it comes to pass, you shall acquire followers. On the next full moon at the same moment in the day, the dolphins and whales will drive the fish from the Mother and on the shores of these same cities. This you will also predict. More will join your cause. Each full moon thereafter, you will predict this same occurrence until you have the necessary power to force change, and bring an end to the poisoning of the Mother and the Father. If your tribe refuses, then the dolphins and whales will continue to drive the fish from the sea until it is barren. If your tribe has not responded, then in a final act every dolphin and whale will cast themselves upon the shores of the Father. These acts would be in vain if it were not known exactly why they were taking place. It is given to you to communicate them."

"I am near death," thinks Messias. "How is it possible for me to return to my people?"

"One of your tribe is being directed to this position. They will arrive soon."

"You have the power to direct a helmsman?"

"Not usually. Your tribe have destinations. Their minds are filled with purpose. Our influence is subtle and cannot penetrate the turmoil. We can direct those whose minds are empty or at rest: a fisherman who wanders, a helmsman in half sleep."

Messias is unsure if he wants to return, he has surrendered to his death and is not prepared to re-enter the world of man.

"You must return," comes the voice. "Time is short. There will be no one else. It is for every creature that has died, and for every creature that is alive, and those yet unborn. It is for the harmony of all tribes, and the peace that has been absent from the Father. It is for the rebirth of your song, and the celebration of the gift of life. The boat comes."

❖ 17 ❖

THE DISTANT THROB OF AN ENGINE awoke Messias as from a deep sleep. The voice of the whale still vibrated in his chest.

In the twilight, a whitewashed trawler with green gunwales came to a standstill a hundred and fifty yards from the brown form of Messias. The boat pitched gently in the light swells. Three men came forward and stood at the bow. The dark form lay low and indistinguishable in the water. A rifle was raised and a shot echoed across miles of purple water. The slug hit the water a foot in front of the form and skipped over it.

"Fallaste', el Tiburon, todavia esata' alla?" The rifle was raised again. Before another shot could be fired, a fin whale surfaced between the boat and the mistaken prey. The man with the rifle lowered it. In a few moments three dolphin came around the whale, bearing a man on their backs. They reached the side of the boat, and one of the men crossed himself, then leaned over and helped the others lift Messias aboard.

"Agua," said Messias in a thin voice. One of the men left and returned with a cup of water. He held it to Messias's lips while supporting him at the shoulders. Messias drank it down. "Mas," and the man left for another cup.

The three dolphin and the whale swam southeast when Messias was safely aboard. The man who had crossed himself watched them dive, and waited for them to come up for a breath, but in the fading light did not catch sight of them again.

The third man had gone forward to the cabin, and Messias could hear him speaking in Spanish on the radio. When he was through he went to the helm, put the boat in gear and swung south.

The two men lifted Messias from the deck and carried him to a bunk. They covered him with an unwashed blanket that smelled of sea death. One man stayed with him and gave him water.

Messias fell asleep and was awakened later at the sound of a loud, high pitched exhaust. There was a banging of gunwales, and then the sunburned face of an American wearing a long billed fishing cap was bending over him saying, "Looks like you've seen some hard days, bud. We'll have you outta here and in a hospital in a couple of hours." The man leaned out the cabin door. "John, I'm going to need a hand with this guy. He can't make it on his own."

A large, gray man in his fifties appeared, and he and the man in the cap lifted Messias from the bunk. Draping an arm across their shoulders, they half carried him to the side of the boat. A Mexican deckhand, a boy in his early teens, stood aboard the American marlin boat and was conversing in Spanish with one of the sharkers. The American with the cap called to him, "Hey, Alberto, give us a hand here," and the three hefted Messias across the gunwales. The inboard cabin lights and aft deck lights glared brightly against the night, and the gray man instructed the others to take Messias below to the V-berth.

The boats separated and the marlin boat surged forward at full throttle. "My name is Tom Masters," said the man in the cap. "We'll have you in a hospital in Mazatlan in no time."

Messias nodded, "How far?"

"We're less than two hours. We'll radio ahead and see if we can't have an ambulance or somebody waiting for you at the dock." The gray man came below and Masters introduced him as John Grant.

Although large of frame, Messias appeared frail laying dark and small on the oversized berth in the plush surroundings. Grant scrutinized him for a long time before saying, "What's your name, fella?"

Hoarsely, Messias said, "Ray Messias."

"Can we get you anything, Ray?"

"Thirsty."

"Alberto", called out Grant, "bring a large glass of water." Alberto returned and handed the water directly to Messias who was helped to a reclining position against the large pillows that leaned against the bulkhead.

"How long have you been out there Ray?"

"Don't know. What day is it?" replied Messias between gulps of water.

"It's Saturday."

Messias took another swallow.

"About a week."

"What the hell happened out there," asked Grant.

"Maybe we ought to let the guy rest," said Masters taking the empty glass from Messias.

Grant looked coldly at Masters and said in a flat voice, "I want to hear what he has to say." Then turning to Messias, he smiled. "How about it, Ray."

Messias felt he was on the threshold of passing out; he wanted nothing more than to sleep. Grant waited expectantly above him. Messias could see that he was unaccustomed to waiting and so to gain solitude he told the story in brief; the amberjack, swept off Cerralvo, the shark attacks, the sail fish, McCorkin's death, the building of the boat. When it came time to speak of the dolphins and the whale he was exhausted and made no mention of them.

The brown and anxious face of young Alberto leaned forward and in broken English said that the sharkers had told him that three dolphin had brought him to the boat after the biggest whale they had ever seen surfaced to shield him from being shot. "Is this so? Do you remember?"

Messias nodded that he had.

"The whale and the dolphins spoke to me."

"What did they say," asked Alberto in open belief.

Messias told Alberto all that had occurred. Remembering verbatim the instructions of the whale. When he was through Messias closed his eyes. Grant and Masters glanced at each other and then rose simultaneously. Grant instructed Alberto to stay with Messias, and that he and Masters would be on the aft deck. Masters poured them both straight shots of tequila, and handed one to Grant. "That was some story," he said, "all the way from Cerralvo. Hell, that's on the other side of the Gulf. Did the shark fisherman see that jury-rigged boat? Did they mention anything?"

Grant downed the tequila in a single swallow before replying.

"Not according to Alberto. Who knows, anything is possible. He could have come this far on his own; made a boat, speared a sailfish, done all those things. A man can get awfully determined when death is the only alternative. What do you make of that story of the dolphins and whale. The plan to save the earth."

"No way. Hell, the guy's been adrift for a week. He's bound to have gotten delirious. That was a full blown hallucination. I didn't believe a word of it."

"How do you account for the dolphins and whale seen by the shark fisherman?" asked Grant in a curious tone that had Masters move a step back and examine Grant's blue eyes in the deck lights. They revealed nothing.

"There are dolphins and whales all over the place. Christ, we see them almost every hour. These Mexican fisherman are full of sea lore. Every little event becomes a mythical story to impress the landlubbers."

Grant held out his empty glass in gesture.

"Suppose this guy Messias is telling the truth?"

"What do you mean, that he was actually talking to a fish? Come on, John,"

"Dolphins and whales aren't fish, Thomas. Just suppose everything he said was the truth. Think about it for a minute."

Masters poured from the half empty bottle.

"I don't have to think about it. Christ, the guy was out of it! I don't believe he or anyone else can talk to dolphins. What the hell are you getting at?"

"Imagine for a moment that everything he said was the truth. In that light, Messias would become the most powerful man of the immediate future, perhaps the long term future. His influence would substantially change our lives."

Masters finished off his tequila.

"How do you mean? No pollution? No war? Yeah, that would change our lives. Hell, it boggles the mind. I can't imagine what it would be like."

"I can image it," Grant said, almost to himself.

"Well, I guess that's why you're a man of position and I'm your lowly parasitic brother-in-law."

"That's exactly why," said Grant, his voice hard.

"You don't actually believe that story, do you John? Nobody would believe that story, not in America."

"No one would believe it, unless a bunch of dolphins and whales start chasing fish out of the ocean."

"Okay, so what if, for the sake of argument, it is true."

"If it is true, Thomas, then the life of ease you've lived, at my expense, would be over. A crusade the likes of which the world hasn't seen for two thousand years would begin. Such a revolution would make it very difficult, if not impossible to live the life we have been accustomed to living. All of industry that is dependent of the earth's resources: oil, gas, coal, water, lumber, mining; and all of industry that is linked to it; transportation, munitions, communications, hell, everything from banking to cosmetics would come to a grinding halt. In effect the entire world economy would collapse under the weight of such changes. And with it would go the political structures that have long kept those resources available and exploitable. Those of us who have nurtured that system to suit our needs would be dead meat."

Masters waved his empty glass.

"Wait a minute, what are you saying, John?"

"I'm not saying anything, Thomas, merely speculating on the impact that man in our V berth might have on us and the world if he was telling the truth."

"What the hell are you getting at?"

"Simply that we are in a unique position at this moment in history."

"Yeah, and..."

Grant was smiling as though he were having fun, but his eyes were cold and dead, and they made the hairs on the back of Masters neck prick up.

"And", said Grant whose mouth now matched his eyes, "we are in an excellent position of never allowing his story to become known."

Masters looked down at his hands, then filled his glass, and drank it down. His head shook slightly, and his voice was pitched. "Listen, John this is crazy..."

Grant interrupted him. "This would be our best opportunity," he said without a trace of emotion. "It'll never be so foolproof as it is right now. We could suffocate him with a pillow, and say he died on the way in. No one would question it. The guy's half dead already."

Masters wiped his mouth with his sleeve. Grant wordlessly eyed his companion's searching desperation.

"What about the kid, Alberto? He knows the story. He'll tell the guide up at the helm. Are we going to kill them too?"

Grant shook his head in feigned tolerance.

"Nobody's going to believe a Mexican kid who tells a story about a man who talked to dolphins about saving the planet. As you said, these people make a myth out of every little event. It'd never get any further than the bar he tells it in. The guide has been up in the fly bridge and doesn't know what's going on. He saw us lift a half dead man on board. Why should he be surprised if the man dies enroute?"

Masters refilled their glasses.

"You're a ruthless bastard, you know that, but wouldn't dirty your hands in a killing. And I'm sure as shit not going to do it. So that just leaves us with a lot of talk."

Grant was smiling again. "You'd do it, Thomas because you're too weak not to. You've gotten too soft to do otherwise. I don't think you'd be ready to give up the affluent life you've so effortlessly embraced these last fifteen years."

"Well that's where you're wrong, John, finally wrong. Because I'll be goddamned if I'm going to kill anybody for it," said Masters, finding his voice at last.

Grant was chuckling now, the tormenting of his brother-in-law having come to its conclusion.

"Well, you don't have to. In the long run it won't change anything. Because if it is true, somebody who has a lot more to lose than either you or me, and there are plenty of those out there, will have him killed. He'll be too dangerous."

Alberto came out on deck. "He has not opened his eyes for a long time, even when the boat hits hard." There was worry in his voice.

"Check on him, Thomas. Alberto, give me a hand with this fishing tackle, we'll be in port soon. Take the reels off the rods and stow them in the tackle boxes." Alberto diligently loosened the reels from the rods, while Grant stood next to him. "What did you think of the man's story, Alberto? Do you believe he spoke with a whale?"

"Si, he speaks the truth. We talked after you and Mr. Masters left."

"What did he say, Alberto?"

"He say a new life is near. He say that he could see in my face the Great Spirit."

Masters returned to the afterdeck. "Something's wrong with the guy, he's breathing funny, real shallow."

"Leave him be," said Grant, pointing to the lights of Mazatlan, "there's nothing we can do here."

The marlin boat pulled dockside to a waiting doctor and ambulance. After a brief examination Messias was lifted from the V berth and carried to the ambulance.

"Is he going to make it doctor?," asked Grant.

"We won't know until we can make a full examination at the hospital. At present he seems to have fallen into a coma."

During Grant's talk with the doctor, Masters pulled Alberto aside. "Alberto, this man Messias is muy importante. You go to the hospital, stay with him. See that no harm comes to him."

"I stay with him." The earnest eyes of Alberto declared his commitment. "I won't let him die."

The hospital had once been a hotel and retained the dusty, cluttered look of an outdated resort gone to seed. Messias laid in a small room with three others, where a single light on the ceiling gave off ominous shadows that reminded Alberto of his mother who had died in such a room. The smell of vomit and urine and the deep, liquid coughs of a man behind the curtain further attacked his senses, and he held tightly to the bed post to keep from running out of this place of death.

Alberto cared for Messias everyday for three weeks. He bathed him with a sponge taken from the Gulf. He changed his bedding when it became soiled, and he called the nurse when the bottles that fed Messias' arm were empty. At night he slept in the hallway by Messias' door. The nurses called him Santito," the little saint."

On a Wednesday afternoon of the third week Messias opened his eyes while being bathed. He smiled at Alberto, and in a hoarse voice croaked, "I'm hungry."

Alberto dropped the sponge and leaped to the doorway shouting, "He lives, bring him tamales."

The nurse brought soup, and Alberto spoon-fed Messias. Between swallows Messias asked, "How long have I been here?"

"Three weeks," replied Alberto. "You remember the whales?"

Messias nodded, "Yes, everything. We don't have much time now. Soon as I get my legs under me we have to get out of here. I'll need money and clothes. There is a telephone number of a friend in La Ventana. He'll send enough money to get me to the States."

"I will get you clothes. My brother, big like you, would be honored if I would steal his clothes."

Messias pushed away the soup. "Bring me some real food too."

In the time it took to steal his brother's clothes and shoes and load up a plate of tamales, Alberto was back at the hospital. He entered Messias' room and found his bed empty. Running from the room he stopped a nurse who was walking quickly down the hallway. She had seen nothing, but understood that three men, "Americanos wearing sun glasses in this dark place, came and took him away."

"There was a fight?" Asked Alberto.

"No fight. They carried him out, he was asleep."

"Was he sick again?"

"How would I know such a thing," she said bruskly and continued down the hallway.

Alberto took a seat on the hospital steps and lifted a fresh tamale from the covered plate, and attempted to sort out this new dilemma. Perhaps the Americans had come to help. Probably not. What can I do? Nothing. Wait. See if Ray tells the newspapers and the TV. Watch for the whales to come.

For several weeks Alberto studied the newspapers, but there was never any mentioned of Messias or the whales. Three days before the second full moon Alberto decided he should travel to a large city on the coastline. He figured La Paz would be as good a place as any for the whales to come.

Alberto crossed the Gulf in the same ferry that very nearly struck Messias. He arrived in La Paz only to learn that the bay on which the city of La Paz was built was shallow and unsuitable for whales that might range close to the shoreline. Perhaps Guaymas would have been better, thought Alberto, while taking the long walk out to the hooked peninsula that enclosed the bay. Here the water was deeper, and it carried hope as he carried two cans of soda, four tamales wrapped in a towel, and a pomegranate, stolen from an outdoor market.

The moon came up full, glowing like a dead sun, illuminating the bay and peninsula, giving shadow life to all things that lived in darkness. Even the sea, without a whisper of wind, conjured a life, but it was one of profound sorrow. Would the whales come at night? Probably not. What would be their purpose? No, in the morning they would come when the light was low and the eye naturally drifted to the sea.

Nonetheless, Alberto remained alert through the night. Just before dawn an easterly breeze stirred the water across the bay, giving the impression that the sea had come awake and was a living thing that slept and stalked and fed.

When the sun broke the horizon Alberto opened the pomegranate and ate it seed by seed.

Near mid-morning a significant ripple broke the wind patterns across the sea two hundred yards off shore. The water began to separate and a dark object parted the water and then rose higher and became a whale, lifting, in slow motion completely out of the water before crashing down in a tonnage of white water. Alberto stood and cheered and waited for another breach. He scanned the water for other whales and dolphins, but the sea surface settled back upon itself leaving a slick spot, made by the movement of the flukes just beneath the surface. When the whale finally broke for a breath it was heading out to sea. Alberto saw it once more and then did not see it again. This was not what Messias had said would happen.

He did not understand until he was on the Ferry heading back to Mazatlan gazing out across the waters, his mind empty of speculation. Suddenly he knew that the whale had come to deliver a message. Maybe something was wrong with Messias. Maybe the time had changed. He only knew for certain that the whale had brought a message, but he had no idea what the message contained.

In the weeks that followed Alberto daily wandered down to the Mazatlan shoreline and stared out to sea. At first he had come hoping to see a whale, and perhaps receive another message, one that might be understood. But after a week he had given up on the notion and now came simply because there seemed nowhere else to go.

The sea glittered in the high sun and bore ivory gulls from its diamond womb. Alberto watched the gulls rise and fall into the sea, and lost himself in their weavings upon the cumulous filled sky.

"A man could lose himself on a day like this," came a vaguely familiar voice. Alberto turned up and looked into the face of Ray Messias. He blinked the clouds out of his eyes and then jumped to his feet and into Messias' arms. Messias smiled and hugged him. "The nurses at the hospital said that the Little Saint was spending his days down at the beach."

"What happened to you? Why did the whales not come?" asked Alberto.

Messias settled onto the sand next to Alberto. "The whales didn't come because there'd be no point to it if the world didn't know why they had come."

"What happened at the hospital?"

"Three guys came into my room, shot me up with something and I woke up in an isolation ward in some private hospital in San Diego."

"Who were they?"

"I never found out. They kept me there until the day before yesterday. I guess when no whales or dolphins showed they figured it was just a crazy story and let me go." Messias released a long breath and looked out across the water.

"Did they hurt you?" Asked Alberto.

"No, but they taught me something real valuable."

Alberto frowned and tilted his head, obviously puzzled.

"I've got to be very careful next time."

"Next time?"

Messias continued to survey the sparkling water, absently watching the gulls diving. "We have to go back out and get a new time table."

"Talk to the whales again?"

"Yeah."

"Can you do that again without almost dying?"

"I don't know. Maybe. Probably not. We have to find a way." Messias lifted his arm and pointed out into the water. In the center of the diving gulls a fin whale erupted out of the silver sea, its full length cleared the surface, and then it arched and crashed back down in an explosion of white water.

"They're waiting."